GRAPHIC LIBRARY™

NATIONAL WOMAN'S PARTY
Fight for Suffrage

BY EMILY SOHN
ILLUSTRATED BY EDUARDO GARCIA

CONSULTANT:
JAMES DIMOCK,
PROFESSOR OF COMMUNICATION STUDIES
MINNESOTA STATE UNIVERSITY, MANKATO

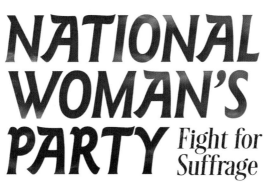

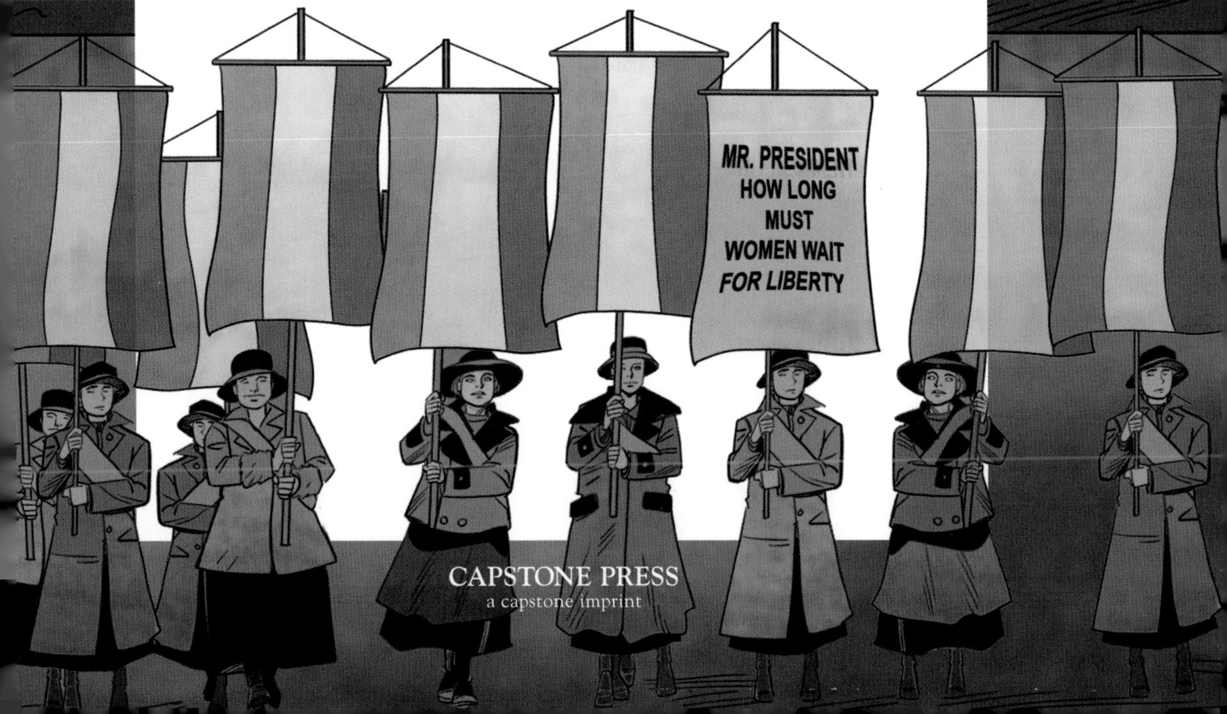
MR. PRESIDENT
HOW LONG
MUST
WOMEN WAIT
FOR LIBERTY

CAPSTONE PRESS
a capstone imprint

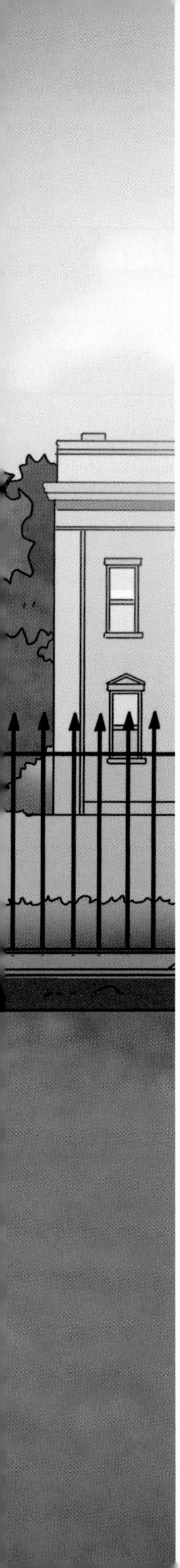

Graphic Library is published by Capstone Press, an imprint of Capstone.
1710 Roe Crest Drive
North Mankato, Minnesota 56003
www.capstonepub.com

Library of Congress Cataloging-in-Publication Data is available on the Library of Congress website.

ISBN: 978-1-4966-8114-0 (library binding)
ISBN: 978-1-4966-8686-2 (paperback)
ISBN: 978-1-4966-8135-5 (eBook PDF)

Summary: On the morning of January 10, 1917, thirteen determined women stood at the gates of the White House and held banners reading "HOW LONG MUST WOMEN WAIT FOR LIBERTY". They were there to force President Woodrow Wilson to take notice of their demand for the right to vote. It was the first day of weeks of picketing, which would stop only when the women were arrested and jailed. Despite criticism from the public and mistreatment by public officials, the suffragists were determined to gain the right to vote. Their resilience and dedication fueled a movement that brought progress to the lives of women.

Editorial Credits
Editor: Julie Gassman; Designer: Tracy McCabe;
Media Researcher: Eric Gohl; Production Specialist: Laura Manthe

All internet sites appearing in back matter were available and accurate when this book was sent to press.

Printed in the United States of America.
PA117

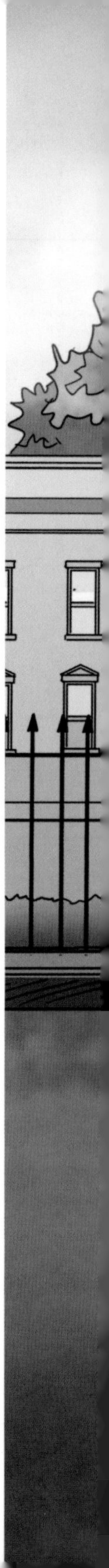

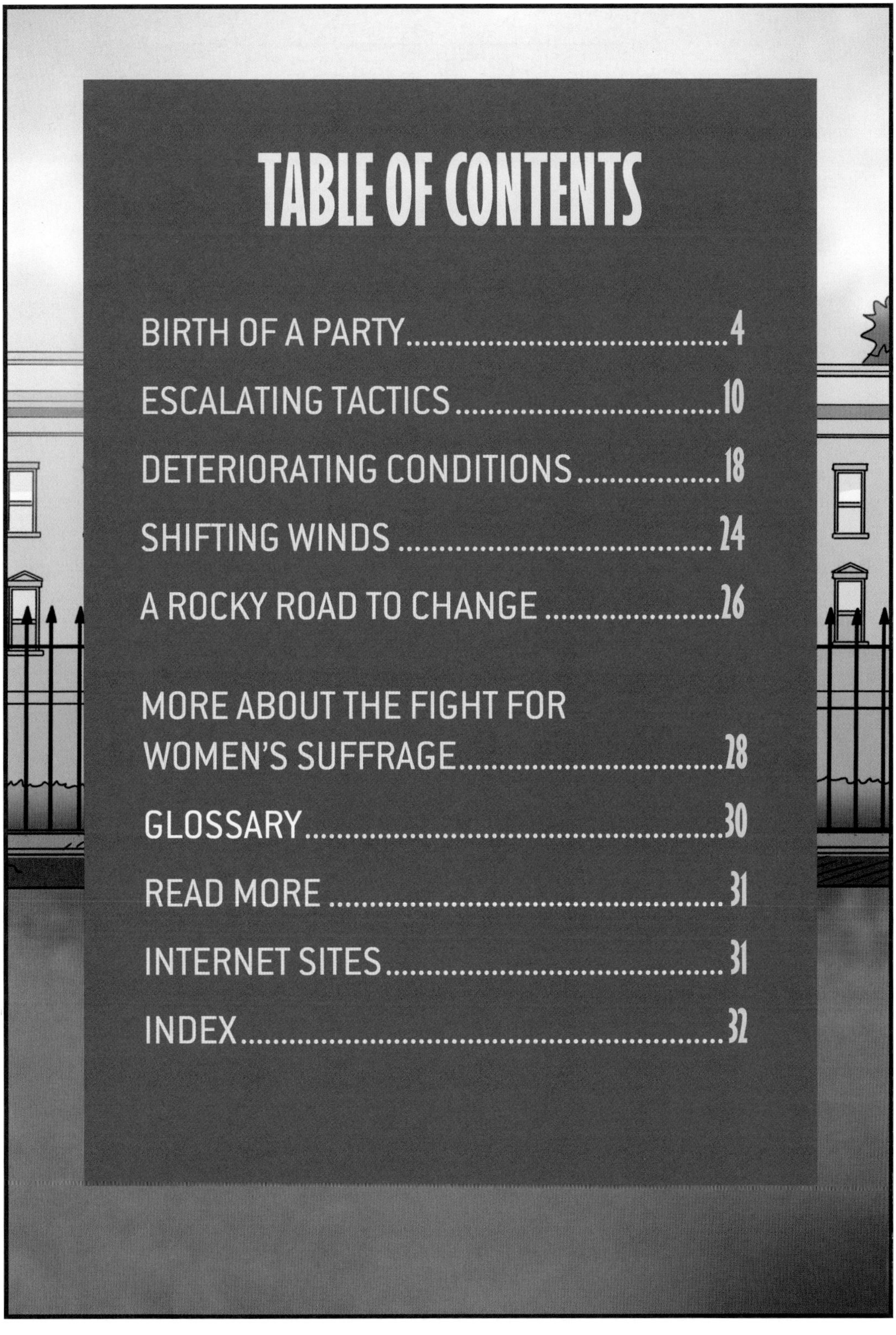

TABLE OF CONTENTS

BIRTH OF A PARTY

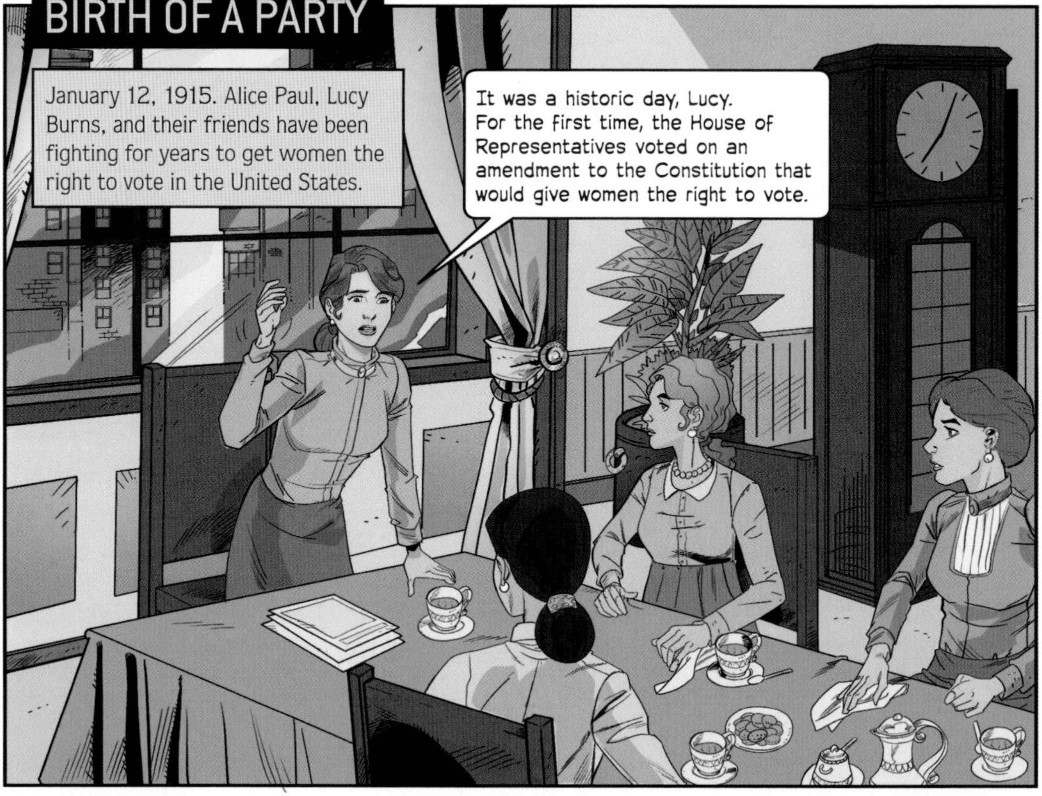

January 12, 1915. Alice Paul, Lucy Burns, and their friends have been fighting for years to get women the right to vote in the United States.
It was a historic day, Lucy. For the first time, the House of Representatives voted on an amendment to the Constitution that would give women the right to vote.

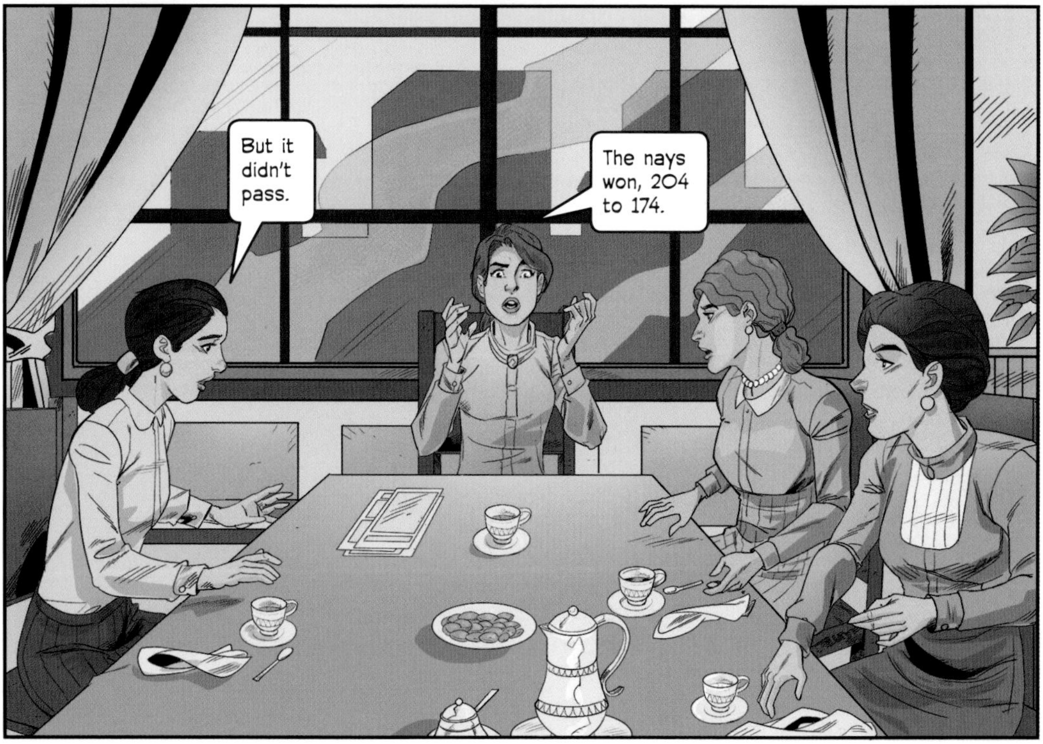

But it didn't pass.
The nays won, 204 to 174.

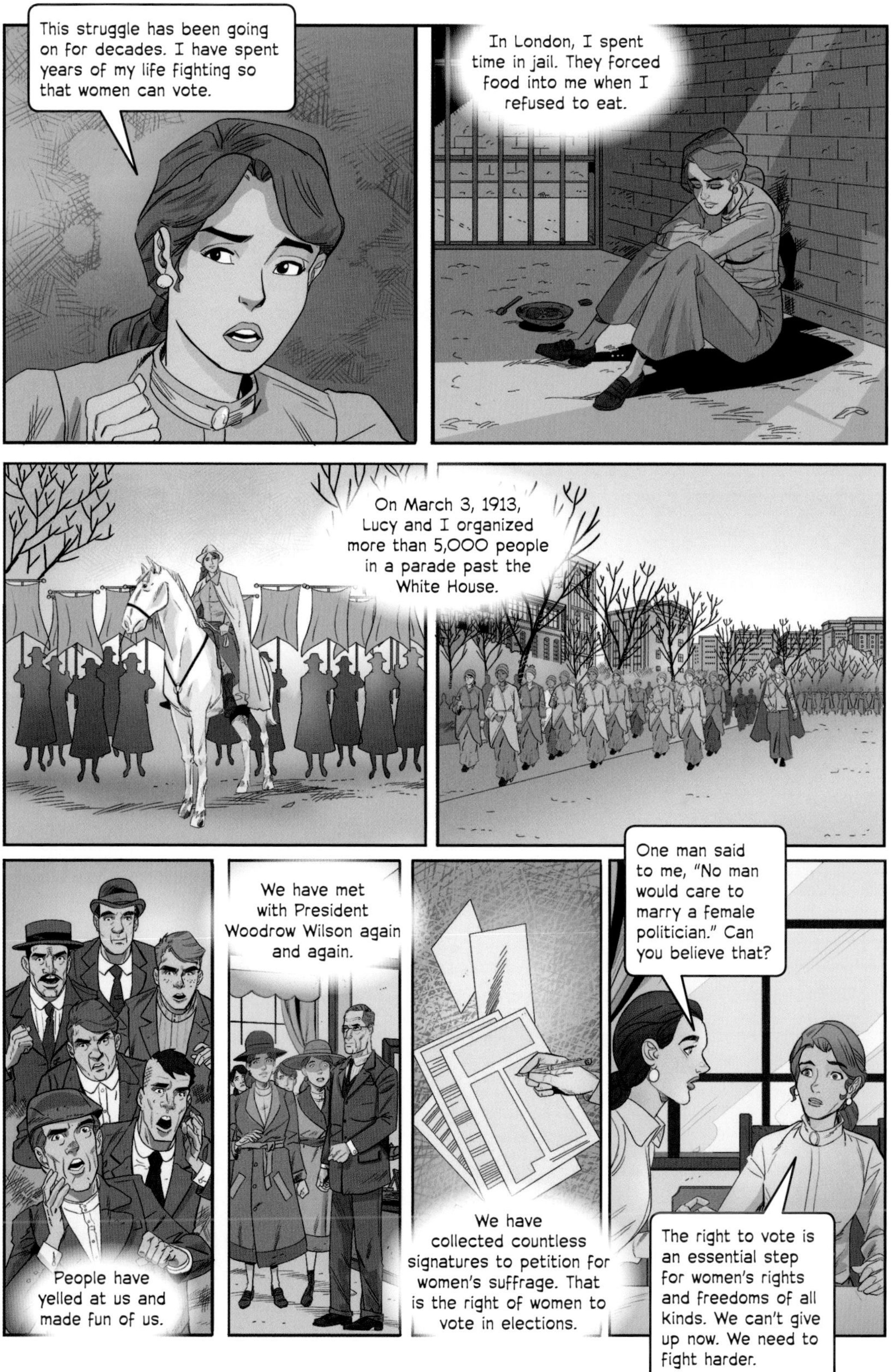
This struggle has been going on for decades. I have spent years of my life fighting so that women can vote.
In London, I spent time in jail. They forced food into me when I refused to eat.
On March 3, 1913, Lucy and I organized more than 5,000 people in a parade past the White House.
People have yelled at us and made fun of us.
We have met with President Woodrow Wilson again and again.
We have collected countless signatures to petition for women's suffrage. That is the right of women to vote in elections.
One man said to me, "No man would care to marry a female politician." Can you believe that?
The right to vote is an essential step for women's rights and freedoms of all kinds. We can't give up now. We need to fight harder.

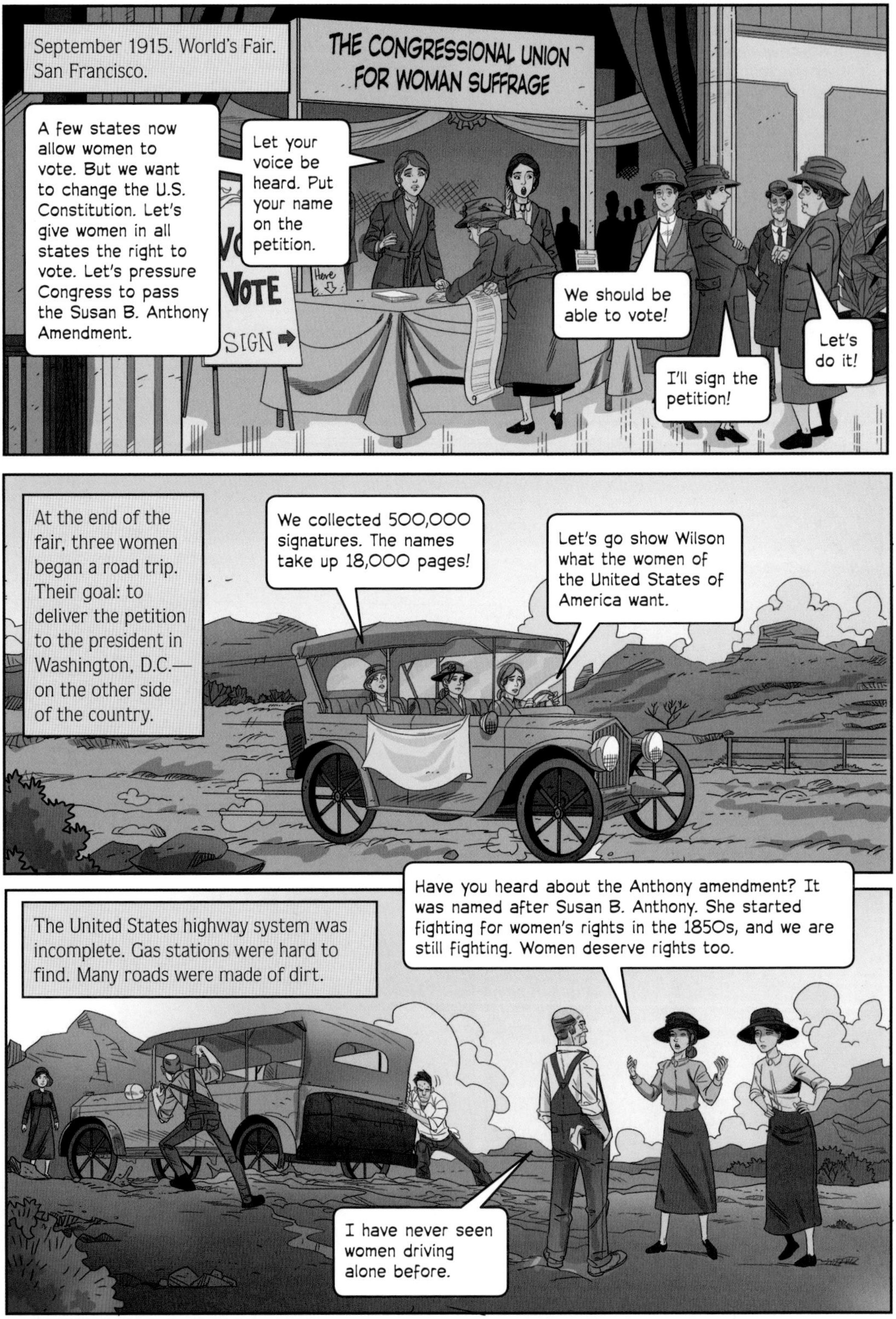
September 1915. World's Fair. San Francisco.
THE CONGRESSIONAL UNION FOR WOMAN SUFFRAGE
A few states now allow women to vote. But we want to change the U.S. Constitution. Let's give women in all states the right to vote. Let's pressure Congress to pass the Susan B. Anthony Amendment.
Let your voice be heard. Put your name on the petition.
VOTE
SIGN
Here
We should be able to vote!
I'll sign the petition!
Let's do it!
At the end of the fair, three women began a road trip. Their goal: to deliver the petition to the president in Washington, D.C.—on the other side of the country.
We collected 500,000 signatures. The names take up 18,000 pages!
Let's go show Wilson what the women of the United States of America want.
The United States highway system was incomplete. Gas stations were hard to find. Many roads were made of dirt.
Have you heard about the Anthony amendment? It was named after Susan B. Anthony. She started fighting for women's rights in the 1850s, and we are still fighting. Women deserve rights too.
I have never seen women driving alone before.

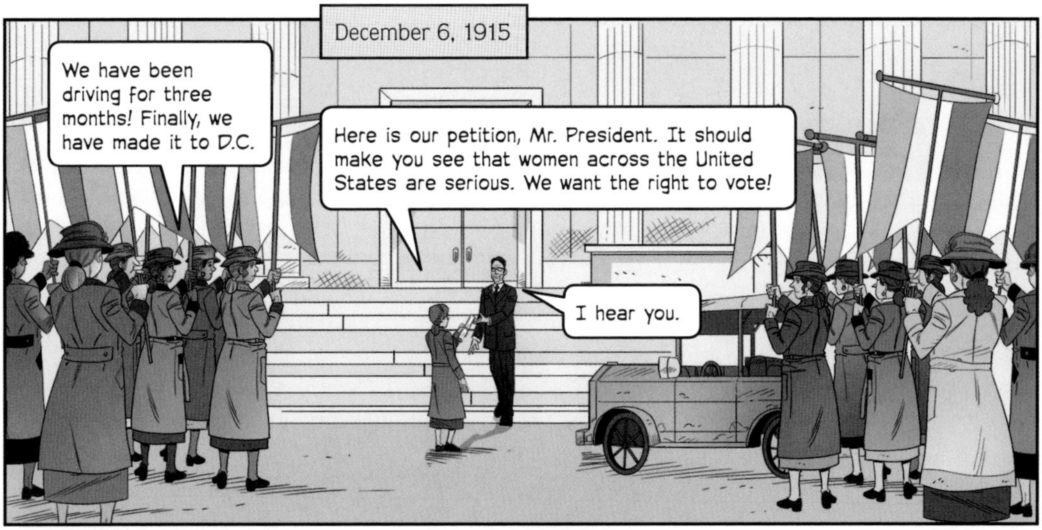
December 6, 1915
We have been driving for three months! Finally, we have made it to D.C.
Here is our petition, Mr. President. It should make you see that women across the United States are serious. We want the right to vote!
I hear you.

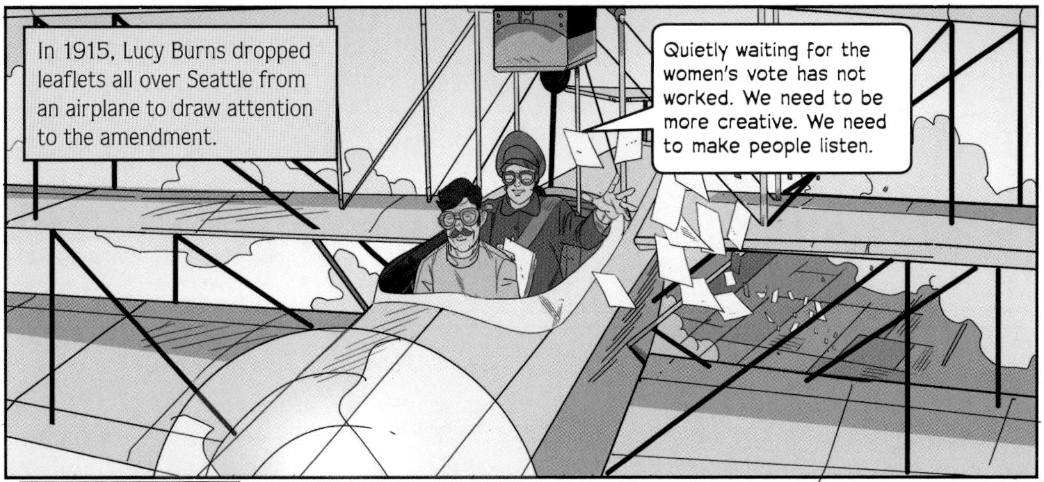
In 1915, Lucy Burns dropped leaflets all over Seattle from an airplane to draw attention to the amendment.
Quietly waiting for the women's vote has not worked. We need to be more creative. We need to make people listen.

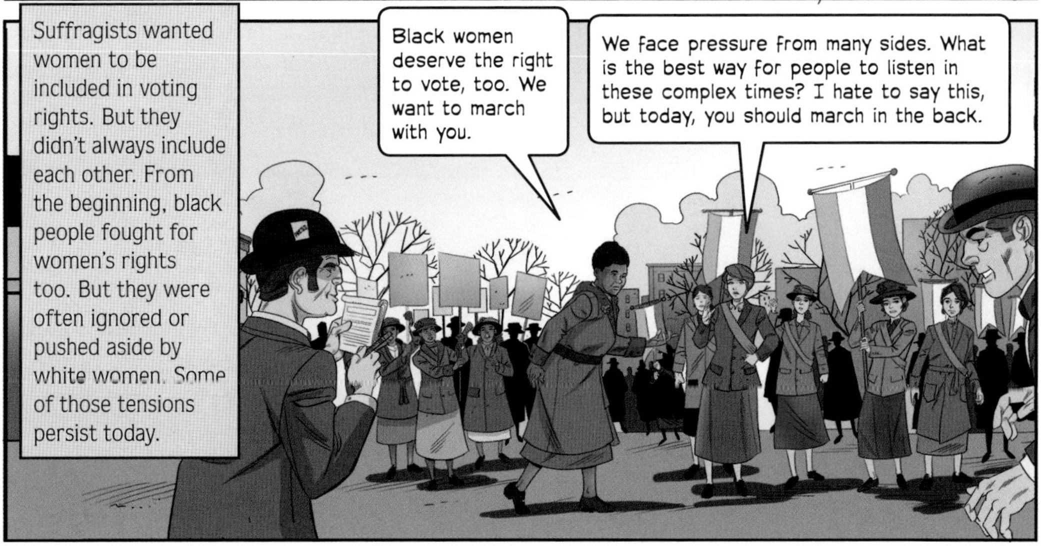
Suffragists wanted women to be included in voting rights. But they didn't always include each other. From the beginning, black people fought for women's rights too. But they were often ignored or pushed aside by white women. Some of those tensions persist today.
Black women deserve the right to vote, too. We want to march with you.
We face pressure from many sides. What is the best way for people to listen in these complex times? I hate to say this, but today, you should march in the back.

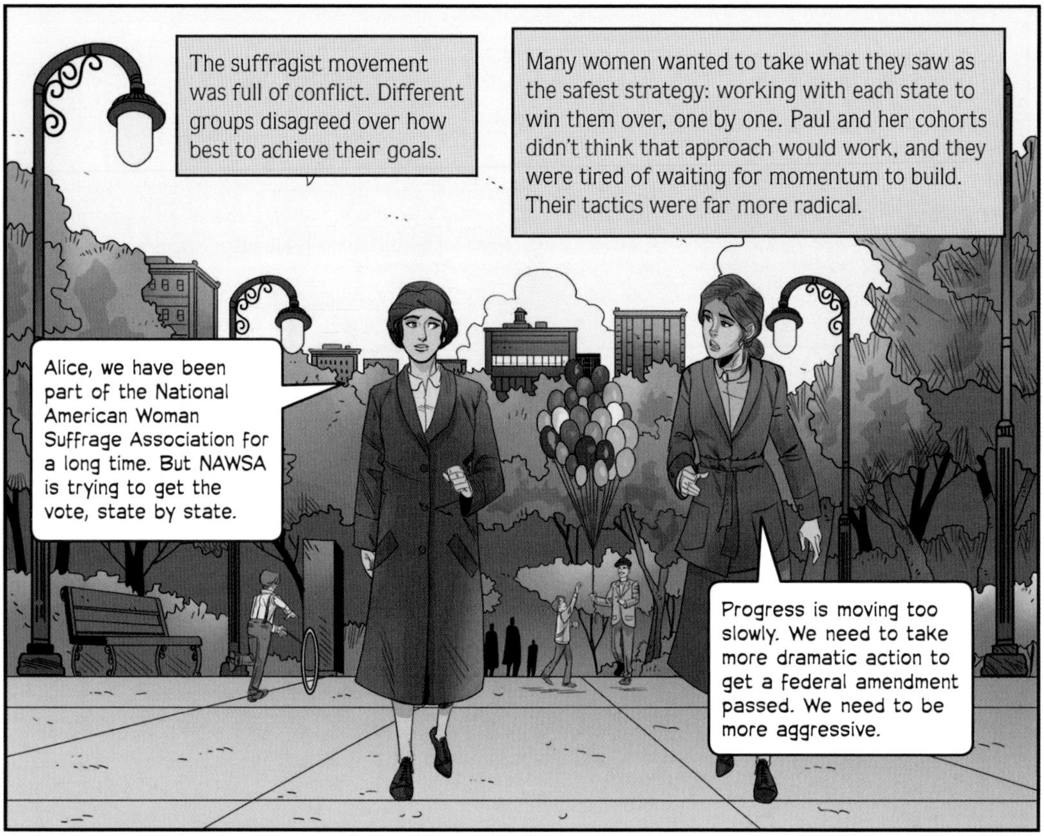
The suffragist movement was full of conflict. Different groups disagreed over how best to achieve their goals.
Many women wanted to take what they saw as the safest strategy: working with each state to win them over, one by one. Paul and her cohorts didn't think that approach would work, and they were tired of waiting for momentum to build. Their tactics were far more radical.
Alice, we have been part of the National American Woman Suffrage Association for a long time. But NAWSA is trying to get the vote, state by state.
Progress is moving too slowly. We need to take more dramatic action to get a federal amendment passed. We need to be more aggressive.

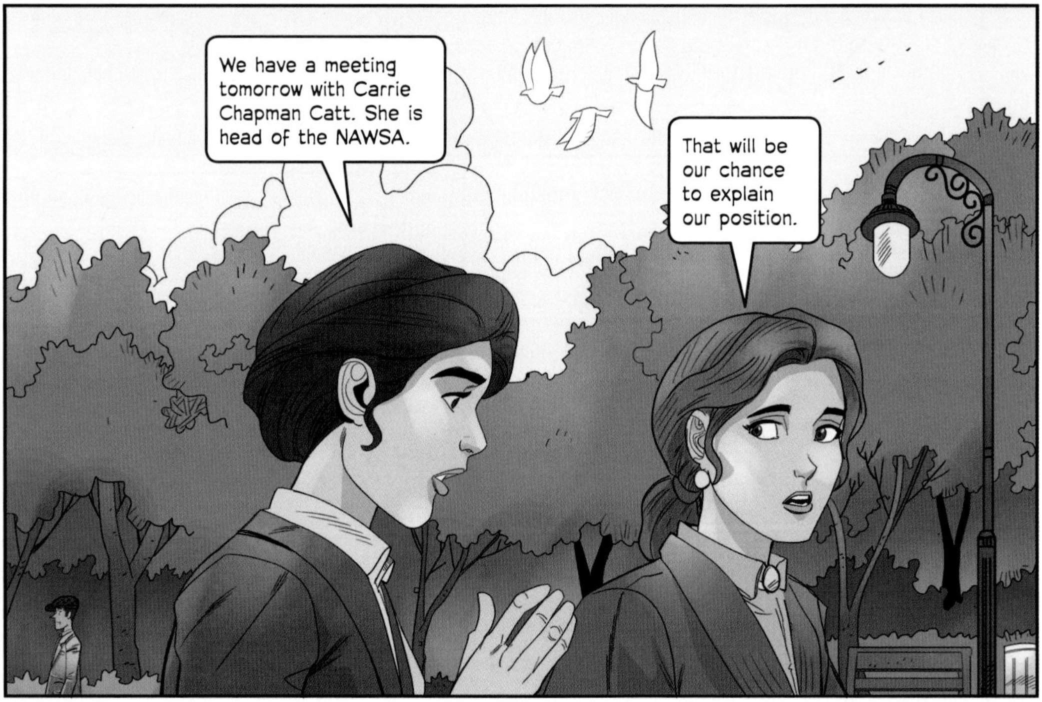
We have a meeting tomorrow with Carrie Chapman Catt. She is head of the NAWSA.
That will be our chance to explain our position.

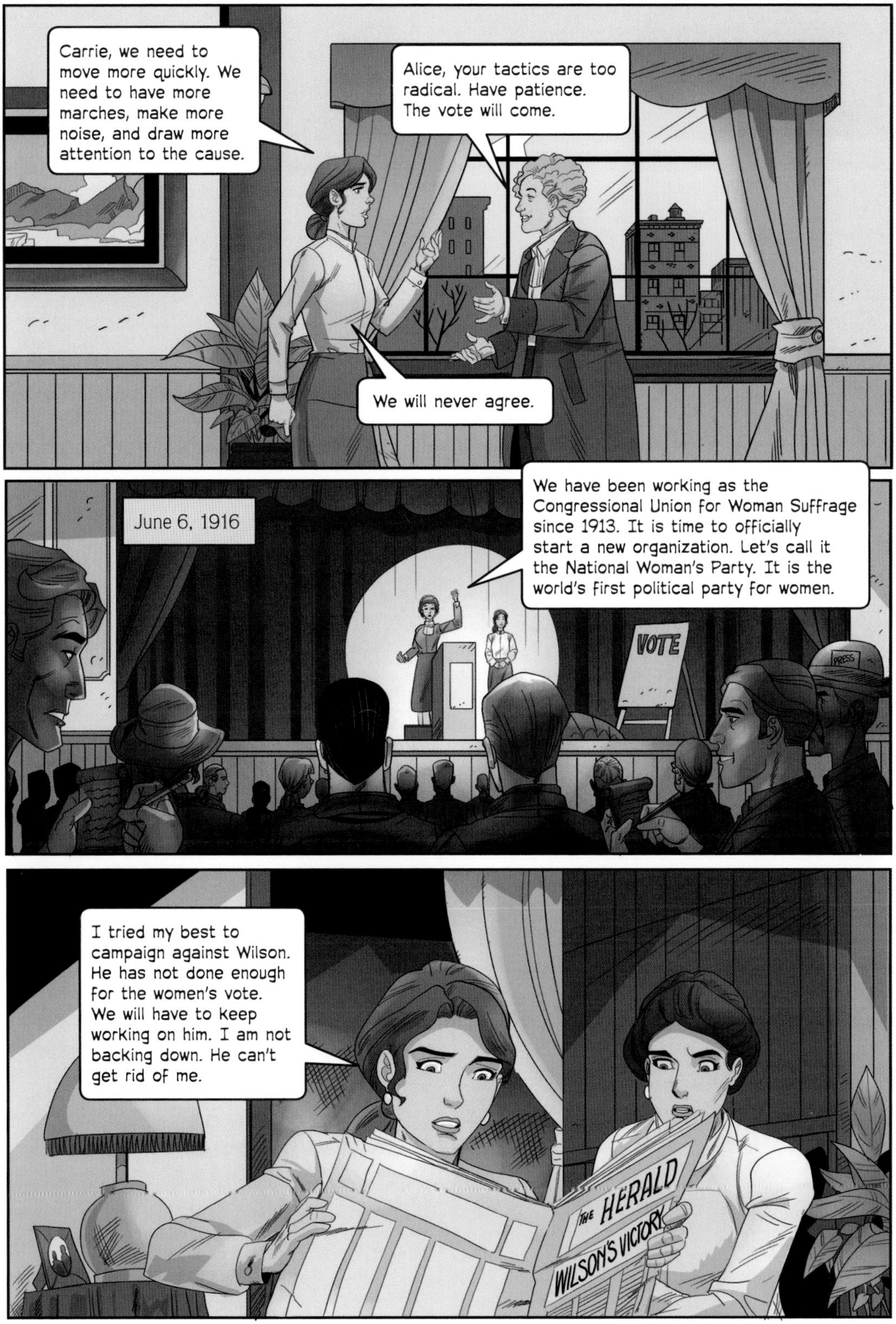
Carrie, we need to move more quickly. We need to have more marches, make more noise, and draw more attention to the cause.
Alice, your tactics are too radical. Have patience. The vote will come.
We will never agree.
June 6, 1916
We have been working as the Congressional Union for Woman Suffrage since 1913. It is time to officially start a new organization. Let's call it the National Woman's Party. It is the world's first political party for women.
VOTE
PRESS
I tried my best to campaign against Wilson. He has not done enough for the women's vote. We will have to keep working on him. I am not backing down. He can't get rid of me.
THE HERALD
WILSON'S VICTORY

ESCALATING TACTICS

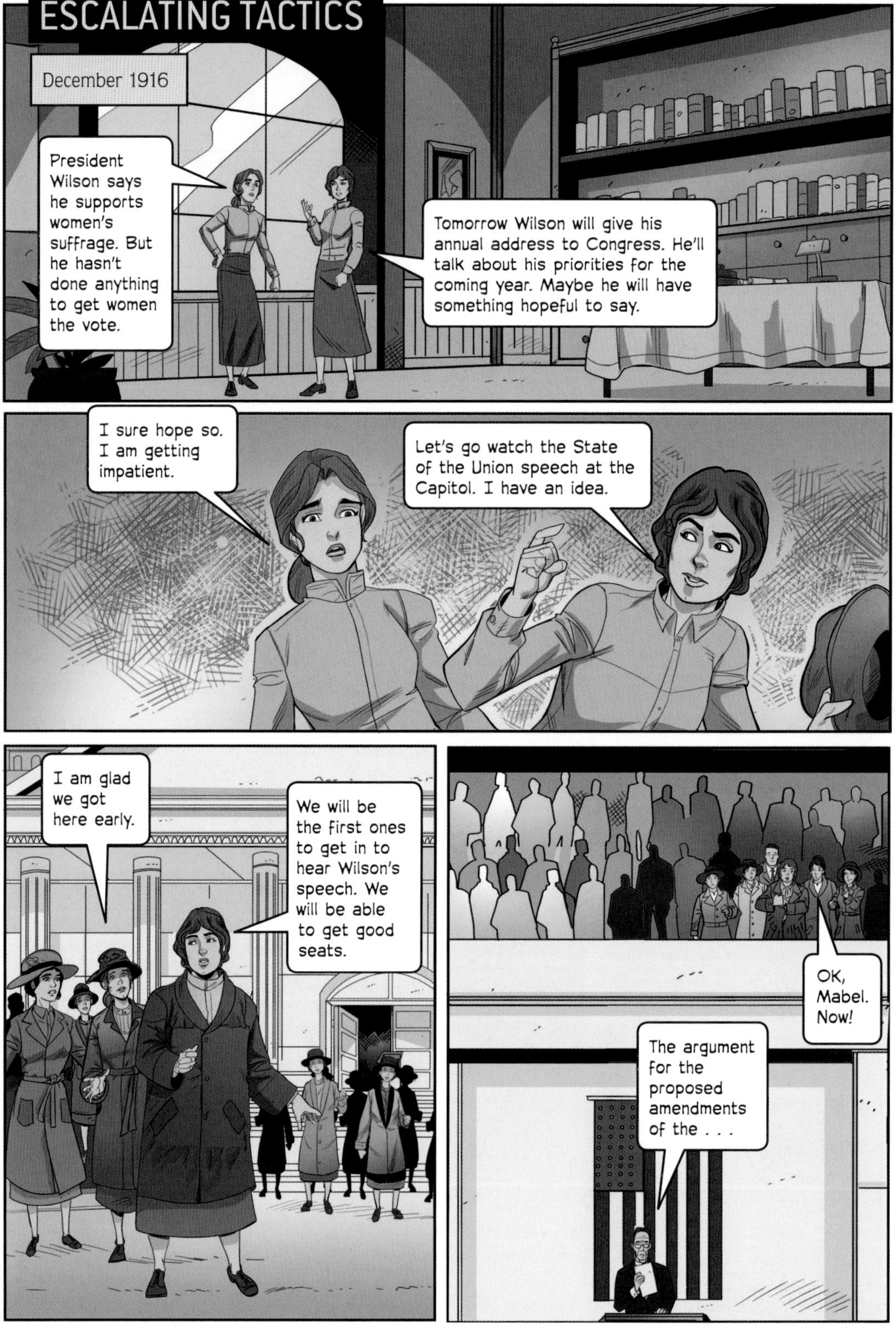
December 1916
President Wilson says he supports women's suffrage. But he hasn't done anything to get women the vote.
Tomorrow Wilson will give his annual address to Congress. He'll talk about his priorities for the coming year. Maybe he will have something hopeful to say.
I sure hope so. I am getting impatient.
Let's go watch the State of the Union speech at the Capitol. I have an idea.
I am glad we got here early.
We will be the first ones to get in to hear Wilson's speech. We will be able to get good seats.
OK, Mabel. Now!
The argument for the proposed amendments of the . . .

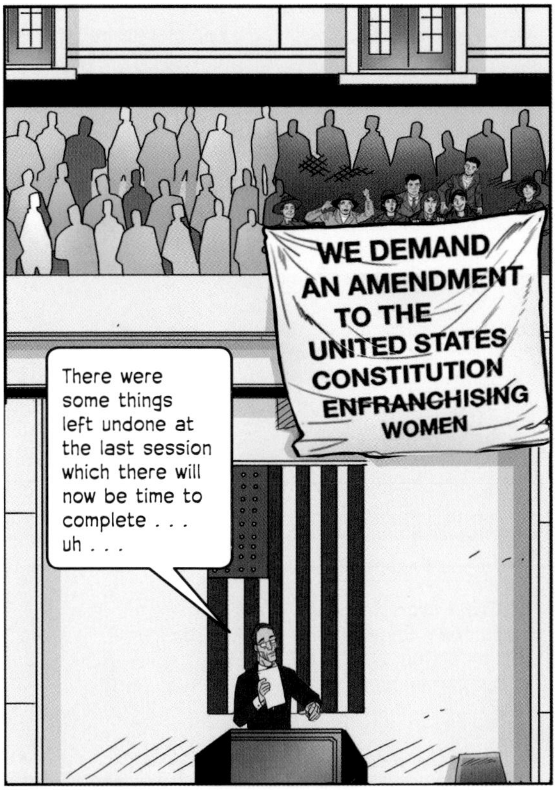
WE DEMAND AN AMENDMENT TO THE UNITED STATES CONSTITUTION ENFRANCHISING WOMEN
There were some things left undone at the last session which there will now be time to complete . . . uh . . .

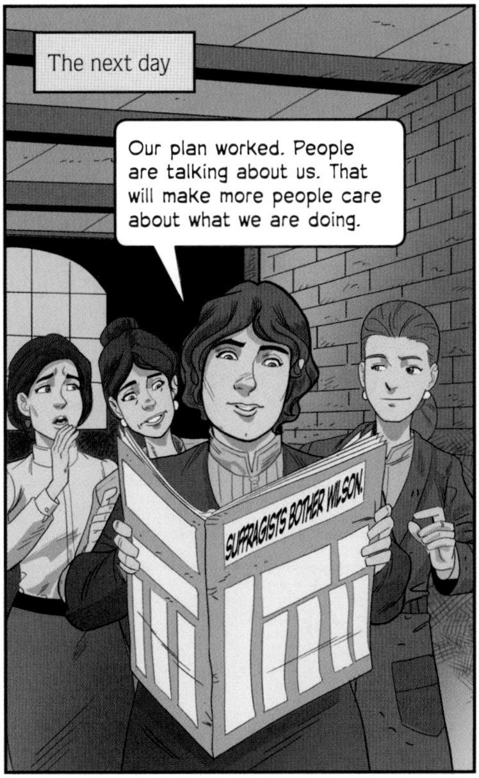
The next day
Our plan worked. People are talking about us. That will make more people care about what we are doing.
SUFFRAGISTS BOTHER WILSON.

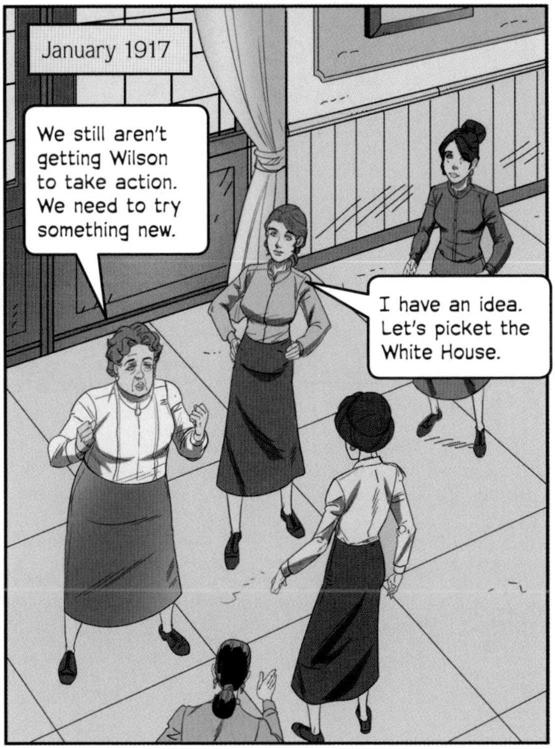
January 1917
We still aren't getting Wilson to take action. We need to try something new.
I have an idea. Let's picket the White House.

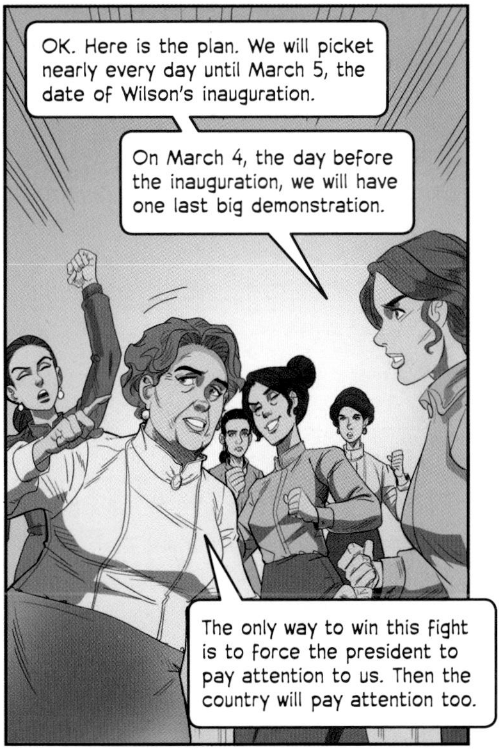
OK. Here is the plan. We will picket nearly every day until March 5, the date of Wilson's inauguration.
On March 4, the day before the inauguration, we will have one last big demonstration.
The only way to win this fight is to force the president to pay attention to us. Then the country will pay attention too.

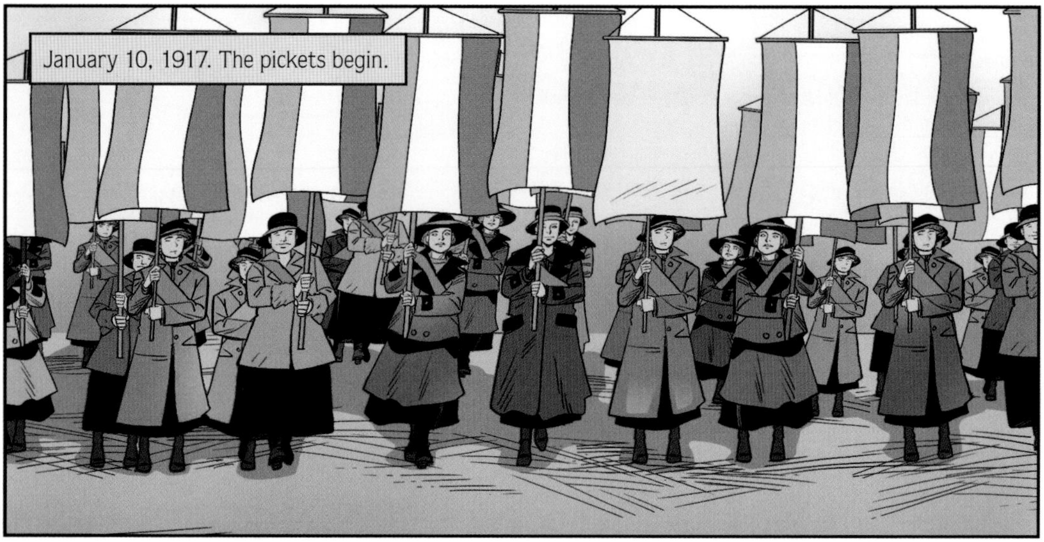
January 10, 1917. The pickets begin.

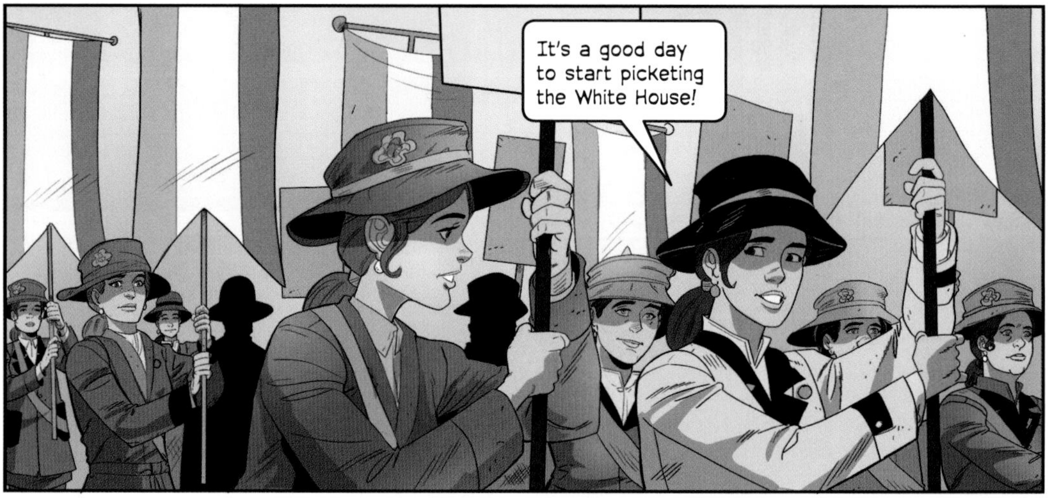
It's a good day to start picketing the White House!

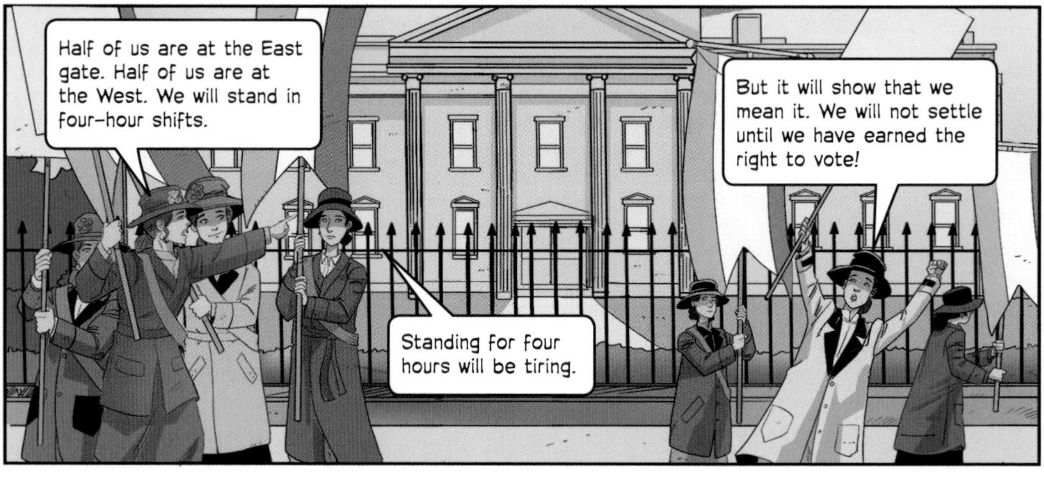
Half of us are at the East gate. Half of us are at the West. We will stand in four-hour shifts.
Standing for four hours will be tiring.
But it will show that we mean it. We will not settle until we have earned the right to vote!

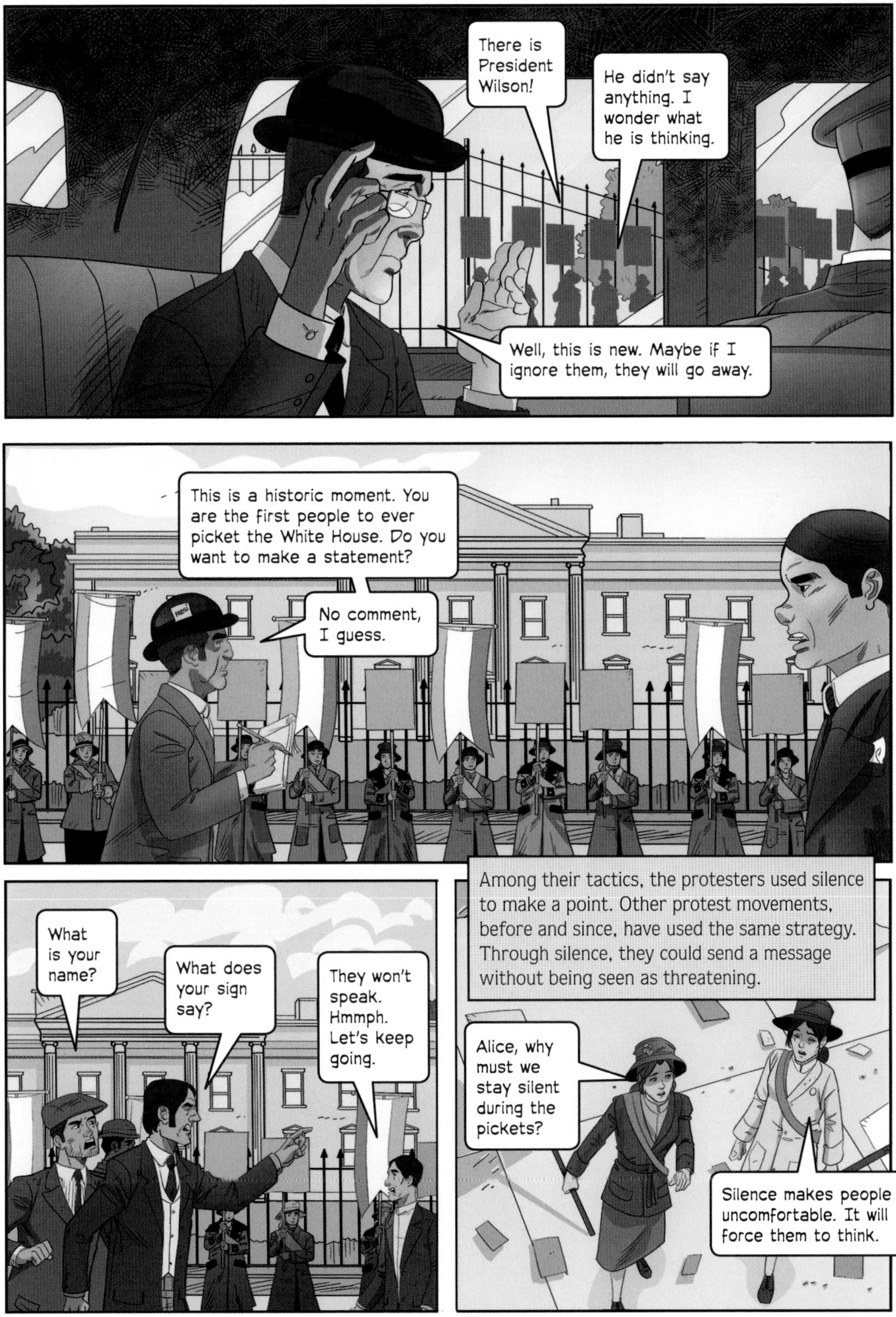
There is President Wilson!
He didn't say anything. I wonder what he is thinking.
Well, this is new. Maybe if I ignore them, they will go away.
This is a historic moment. You are the first people to ever picket the White House. Do you want to make a statement?
No comment, I guess.
What is your name?
What does your sign say?
They won't speak. Hmmph. Let's keep going.
Among their tactics, the protesters used silence to make a point. Other protest movements, before and since, have used the same strategy. Through silence, they could send a message without being seen as threatening.
Alice, why must we stay silent during the pickets?
Silence makes people uncomfortable. It will force them to think.

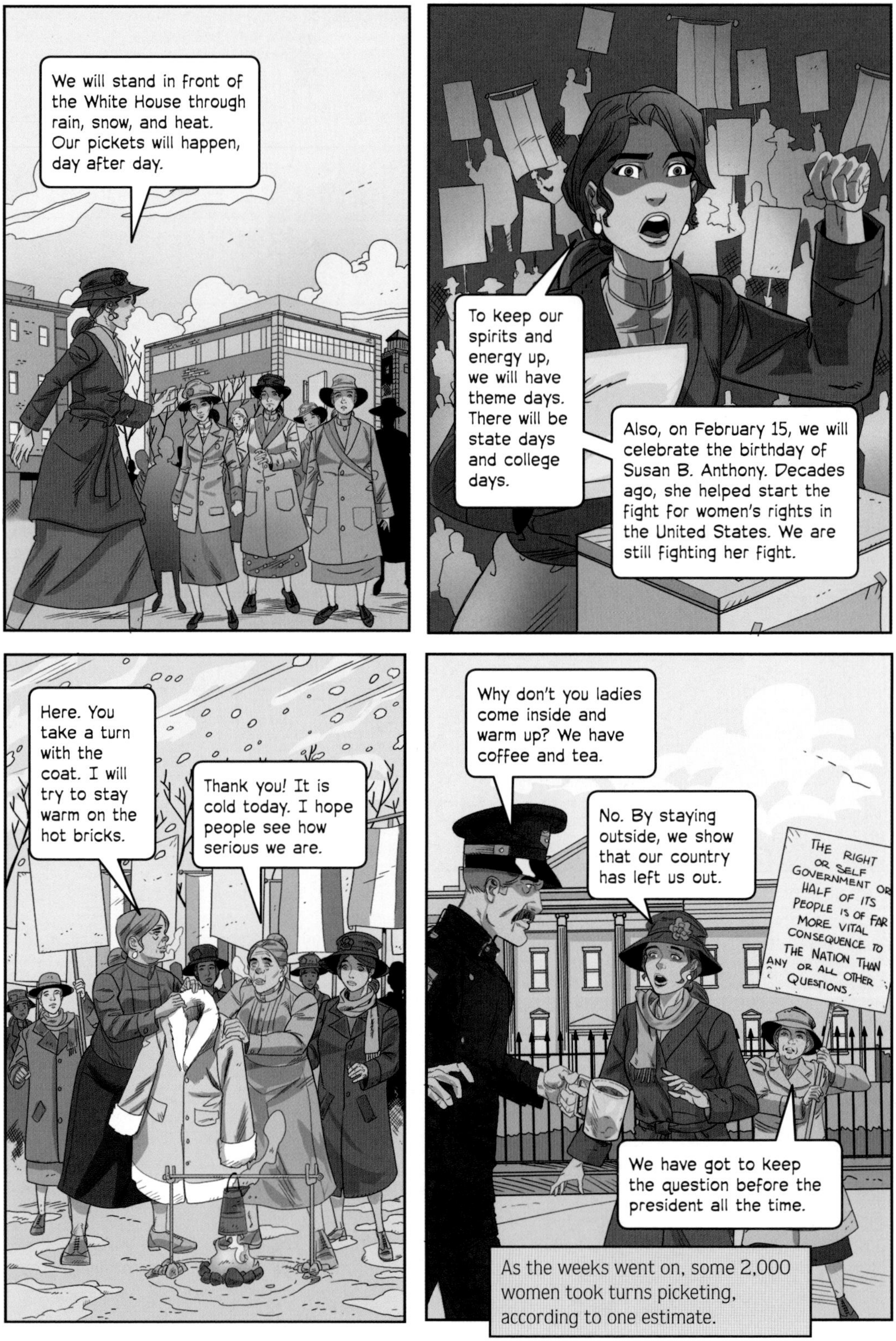
We will stand in front of the White House through rain, snow, and heat. Our pickets will happen, day after day.
To keep our spirits and energy up, we will have theme days. There will be state days and college days.
Also, on February 15, we will celebrate the birthday of Susan B. Anthony. Decades ago, she helped start the fight for women's rights in the United States. We are still fighting her fight.
Here. You take a turn with the coat. I will try to stay warm on the hot bricks.
Thank you! It is cold today. I hope people see how serious we are.
Why don't you ladies come inside and warm up? We have coffee and tea.
No. By staying outside, we show that our country has left us out.
THE RIGHT OR SELF GOVERNMENT OR HALF OF ITS PEOPLE IS OF FAR MORE VITAL CONSEQUENCE TO THE NATION THAN ANY OR ALL OTHER QUESTIONS
We have got to keep the question before the president all the time.
As the weeks went on, some 2,000 women took turns picketing, according to one estimate.

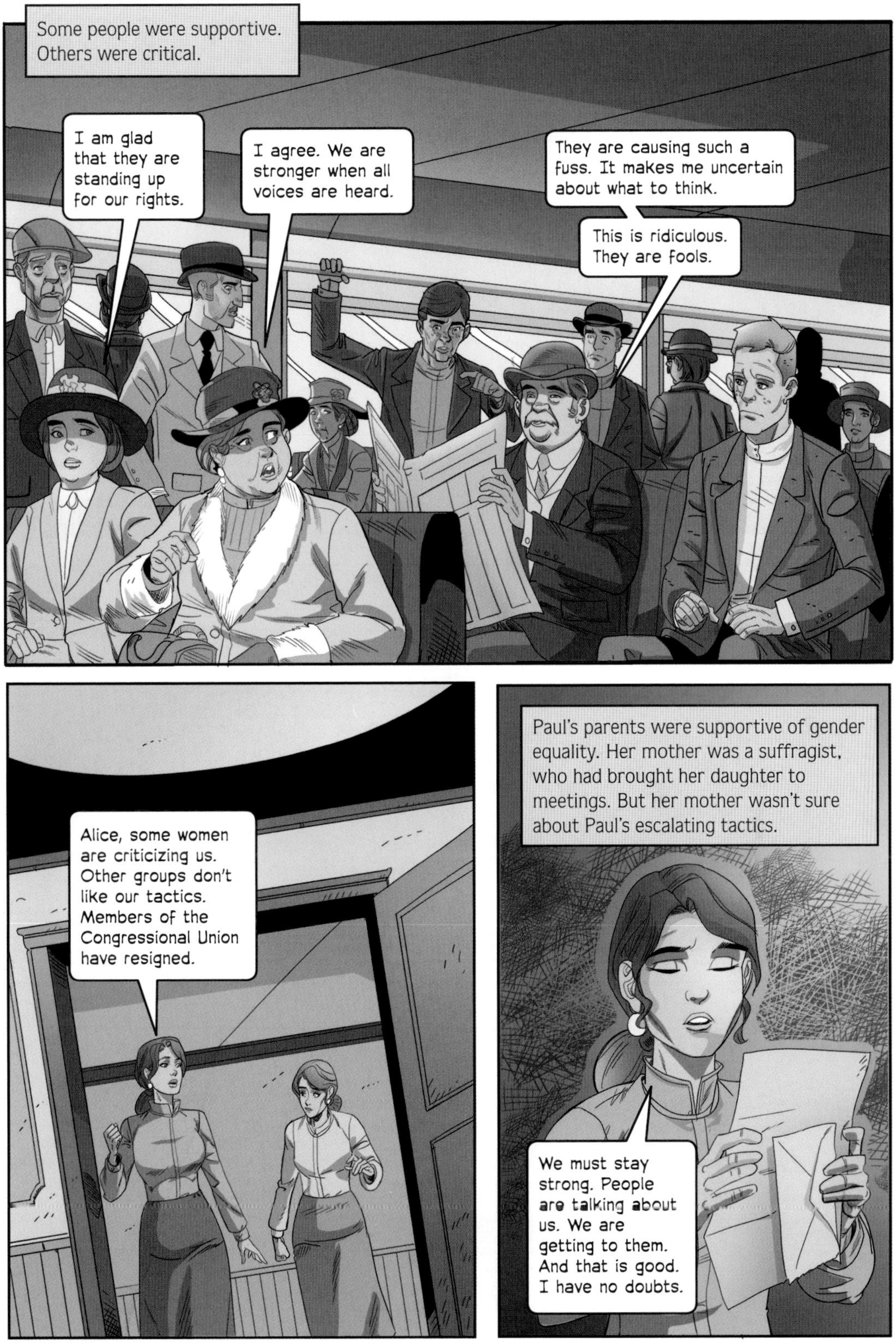
Some people were supportive. Others were critical.
I am glad that they are standing up for our rights.
I agree. We are stronger when all voices are heard.
They are causing such a fuss. It makes me uncertain about what to think.
This is ridiculous. They are fools.
Alice, some women are criticizing us. Other groups don't like our tactics. Members of the Congressional Union have resigned.
Paul's parents were supportive of gender equality. Her mother was a suffragist, who had brought her daughter to meetings. But her mother wasn't sure about Paul's escalating tactics.
We must stay strong. People are talking about us. We are getting to them. And that is good. I have no doubts.

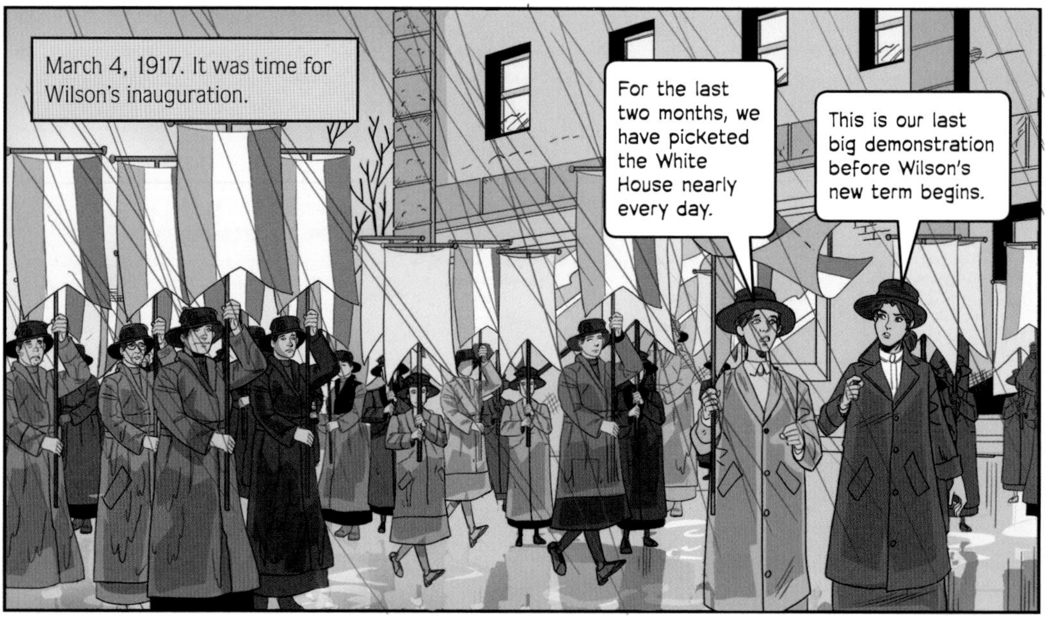
March 4, 1917. It was time for Wilson's inauguration.
For the last two months, we have picketed the White House nearly every day.
This is our last big demonstration before Wilson's new term begins.

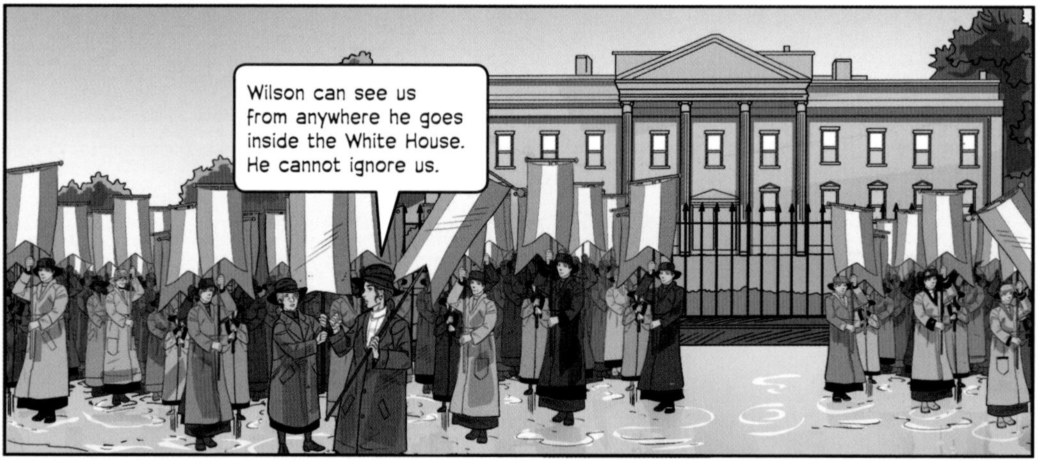
Wilson can see us from anywhere he goes inside the White House. He cannot ignore us.

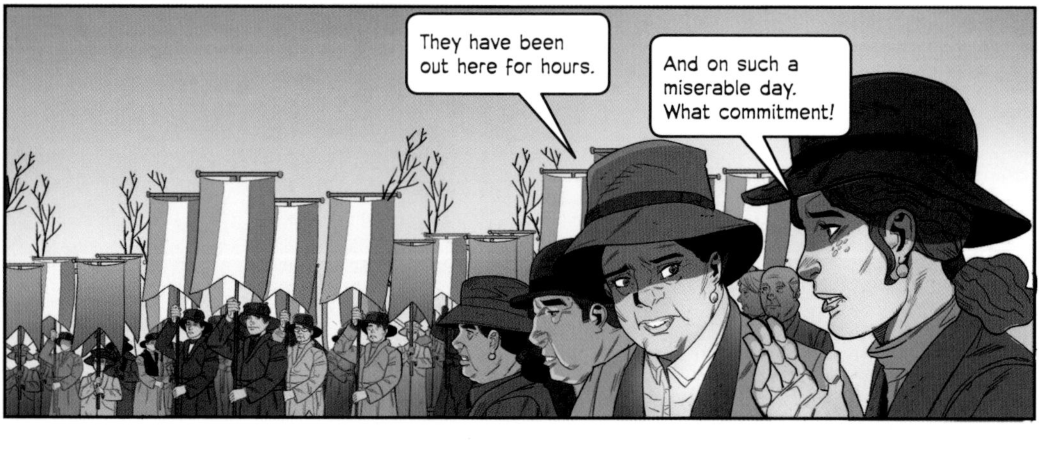
They have been out here for hours.
And on such a miserable day. What commitment!

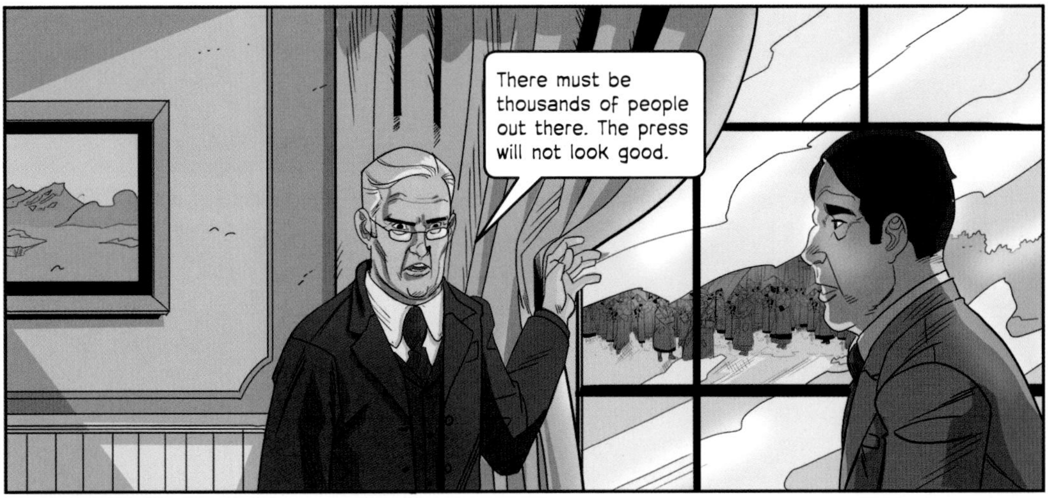
There must be thousands of people out there. The press will not look good.

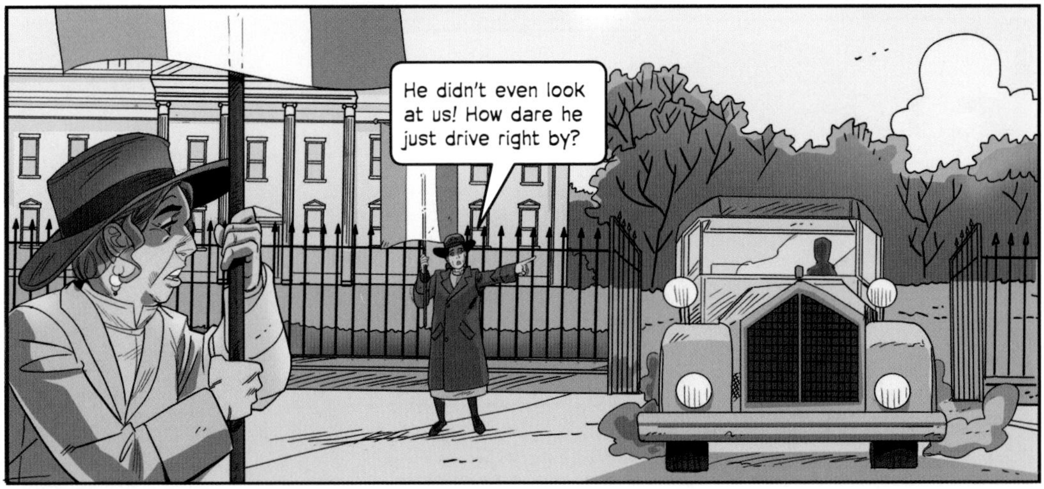
He didn't even look at us! How dare he just drive right by?

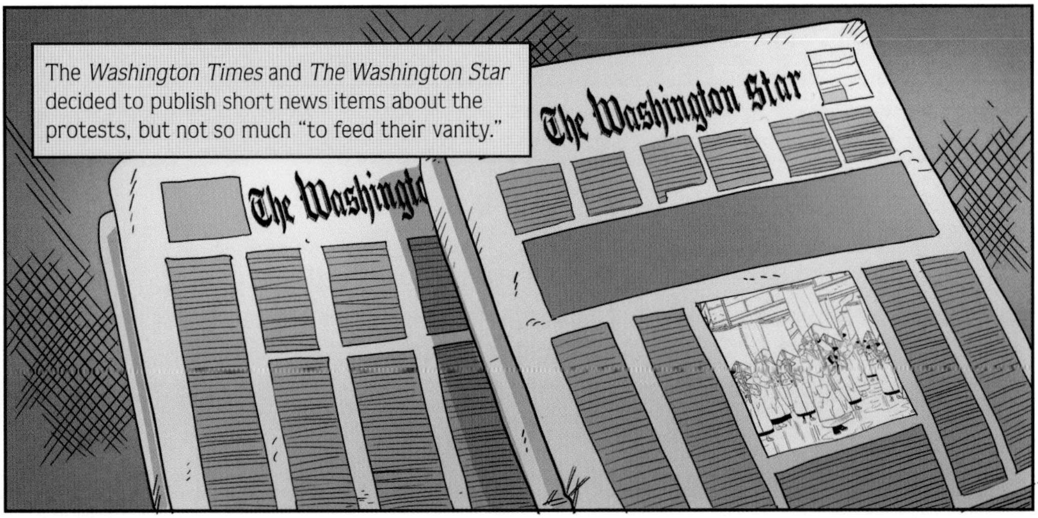
The *Washington Times* and *The Washington Star* decided to publish short news items about the protests, but not so much "to feed their vanity."
The Washington Star

DETERIORATING CONDITIONS

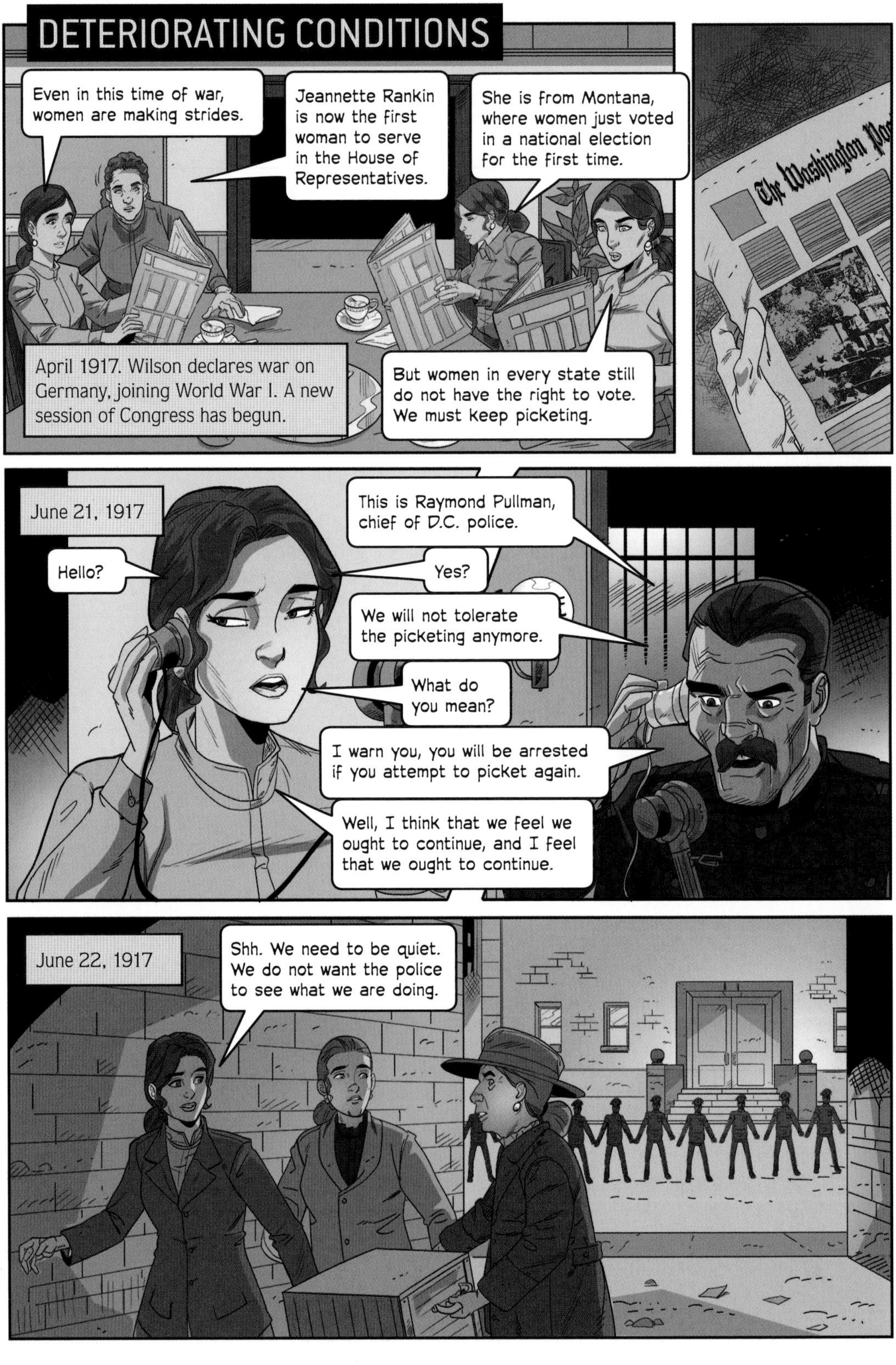
Even in this time of war, women are making strides.
Jeannette Rankin is now the first woman to serve in the House of Representatives.
She is from Montana, where women just voted in a national election for the first time.
April 1917. Wilson declares war on Germany, joining World War I. A new session of Congress has begun.
But women in every state still do not have the right to vote. We must keep picketing.
June 21, 1917
Hello?
This is Raymond Pullman, chief of D.C. police.
Yes?
We will not tolerate the picketing anymore.
What do you mean?
I warn you, you will be arrested if you attempt to picket again.
Well, I think that we feel we ought to continue, and I feel that we ought to continue.
June 22, 1917
Shh. We need to be quiet. We do not want the police to see what we are doing.

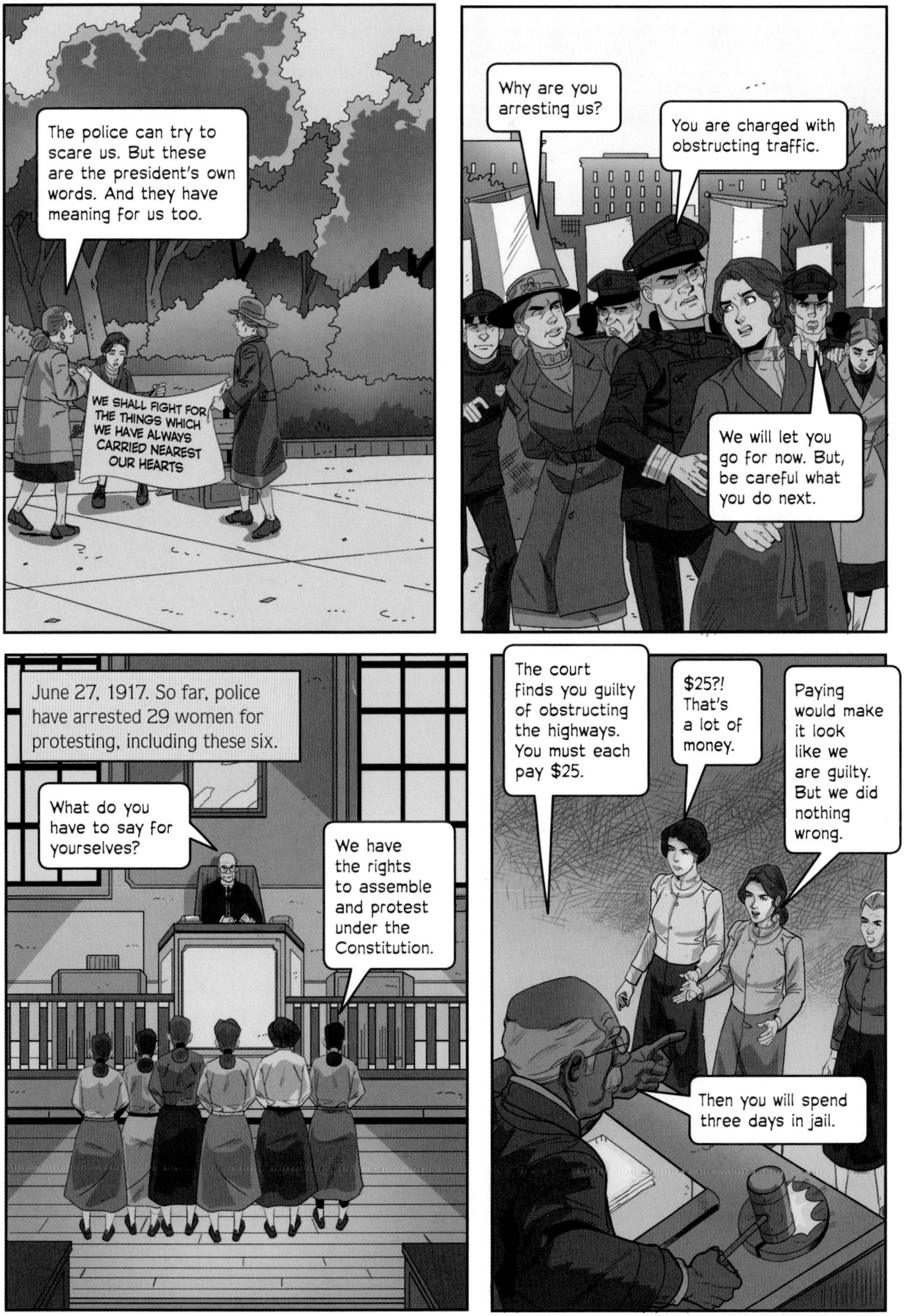
The police can try to scare us. But these are the president's own words. And they have meaning for us too.
WE SHALL FIGHT FOR THE THINGS WHICH WE HAVE ALWAYS CARRIED NEAREST OUR HEARTS
Why are you arresting us?
You are charged with obstructing traffic.
We will let you go for now. But, be careful what you do next.
June 27, 1917. So far, police have arrested 29 women for protesting, including these six.
What do you have to say for yourselves?
We have the rights to assemble and protest under the Constitution.
The court finds you guilty of obstructing the highways. You must each pay $25.
$25?! That's a lot of money.
Paying would make it look like we are guilty. But we did nothing wrong.
Then you will spend three days in jail.

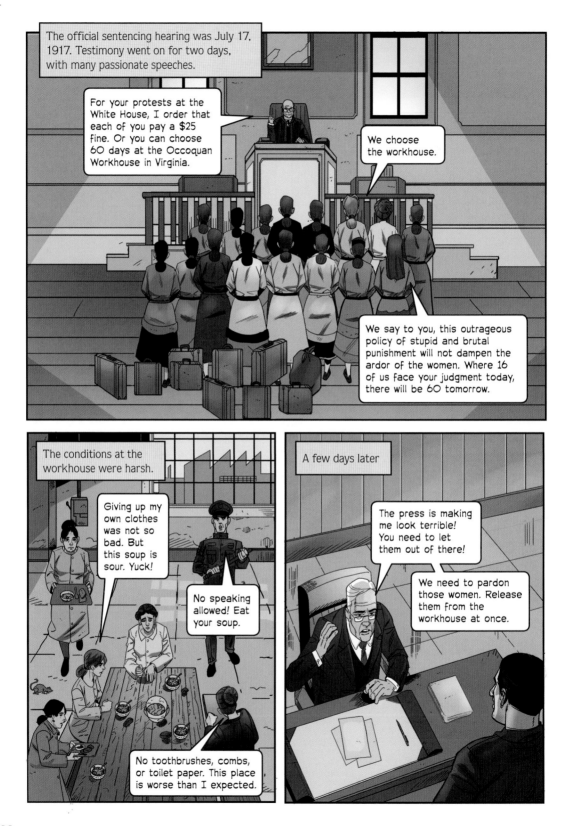

The official sentencing hearing was July 17, 1917. Testimony went on for two days, with many passionate speeches.

For your protests at the White House, I order that each of you pay a $25 fine. Or you can choose 60 days at the Occoquan Workhouse in Virginia.

We choose the workhouse.

We say to you, this outrageous policy of stupid and brutal punishment will not dampen the ardor of the women. Where 16 of us face your judgment today, there will be 60 tomorrow.

The conditions at the workhouse were harsh.

Giving up my own clothes was not so bad. But this soup is sour. Yuck!

No speaking allowed! Eat your soup.

No toothbrushes, combs, or toilet paper. This place is worse than I expected.

A few days later

The press is making me look terrible! You need to let them out of there!

We need to pardon those women. Release them from the workhouse at once.

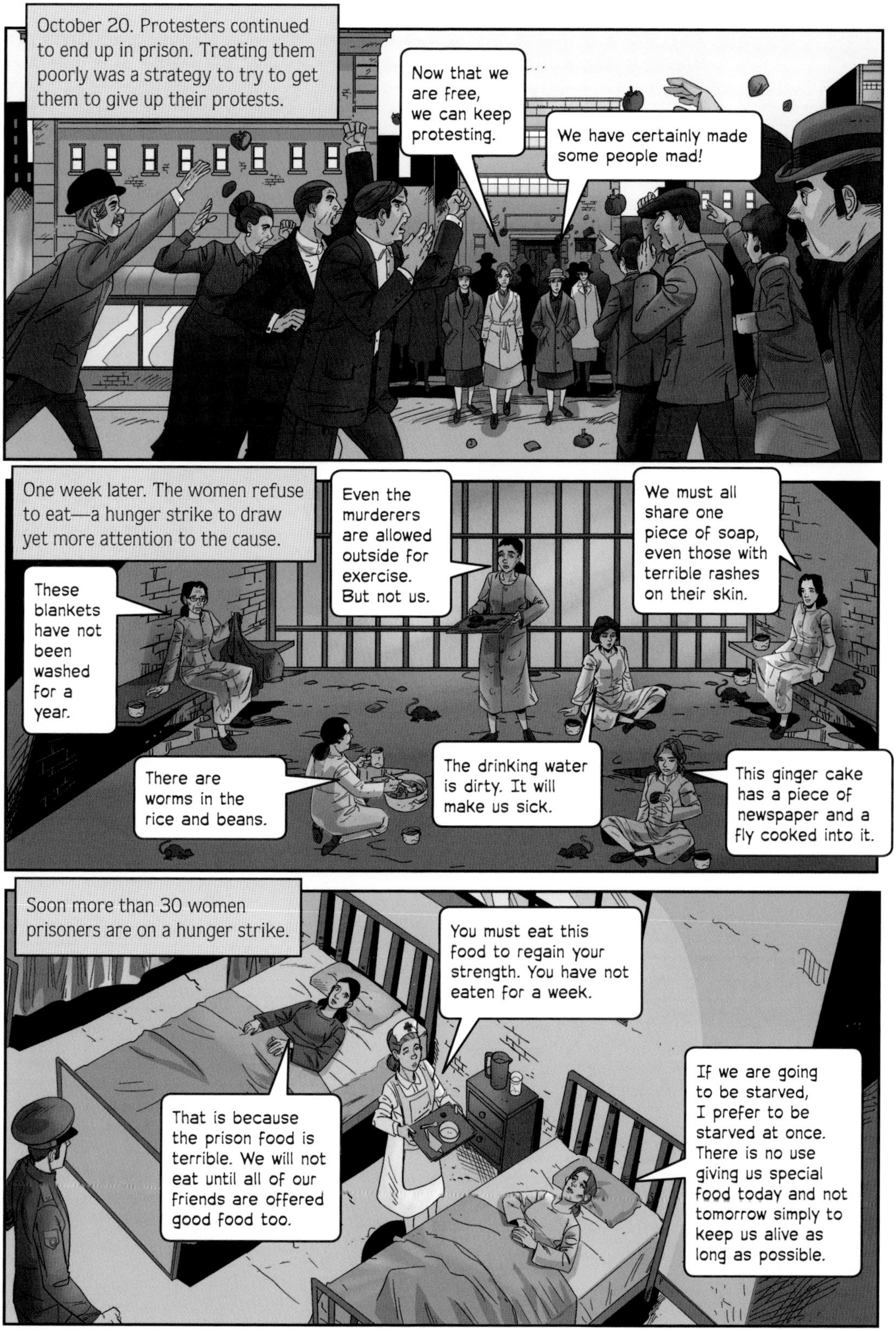
October 20. Protesters continued to end up in prison. Treating them poorly was a strategy to try to get them to give up their protests.
Now that we are free, we can keep protesting.
We have certainly made some people mad!
One week later. The women refuse to eat—a hunger strike to draw yet more attention to the cause.
These blankets have not been washed for a year.
Even the murderers are allowed outside for exercise. But not us.
We must all share one piece of soap, even those with terrible rashes on their skin.
There are worms in the rice and beans.
The drinking water is dirty. It will make us sick.
This ginger cake has a piece of newspaper and a fly cooked into it.
Soon more than 30 women prisoners are on a hunger strike.
You must eat this food to regain your strength. You have not eaten for a week.
That is because the prison food is terrible. We will not eat until all of our friends are offered good food too.
If we are going to be starved, I prefer to be starved at once. There is no use giving us special food today and not tomorrow simply to keep us alive as long as possible.

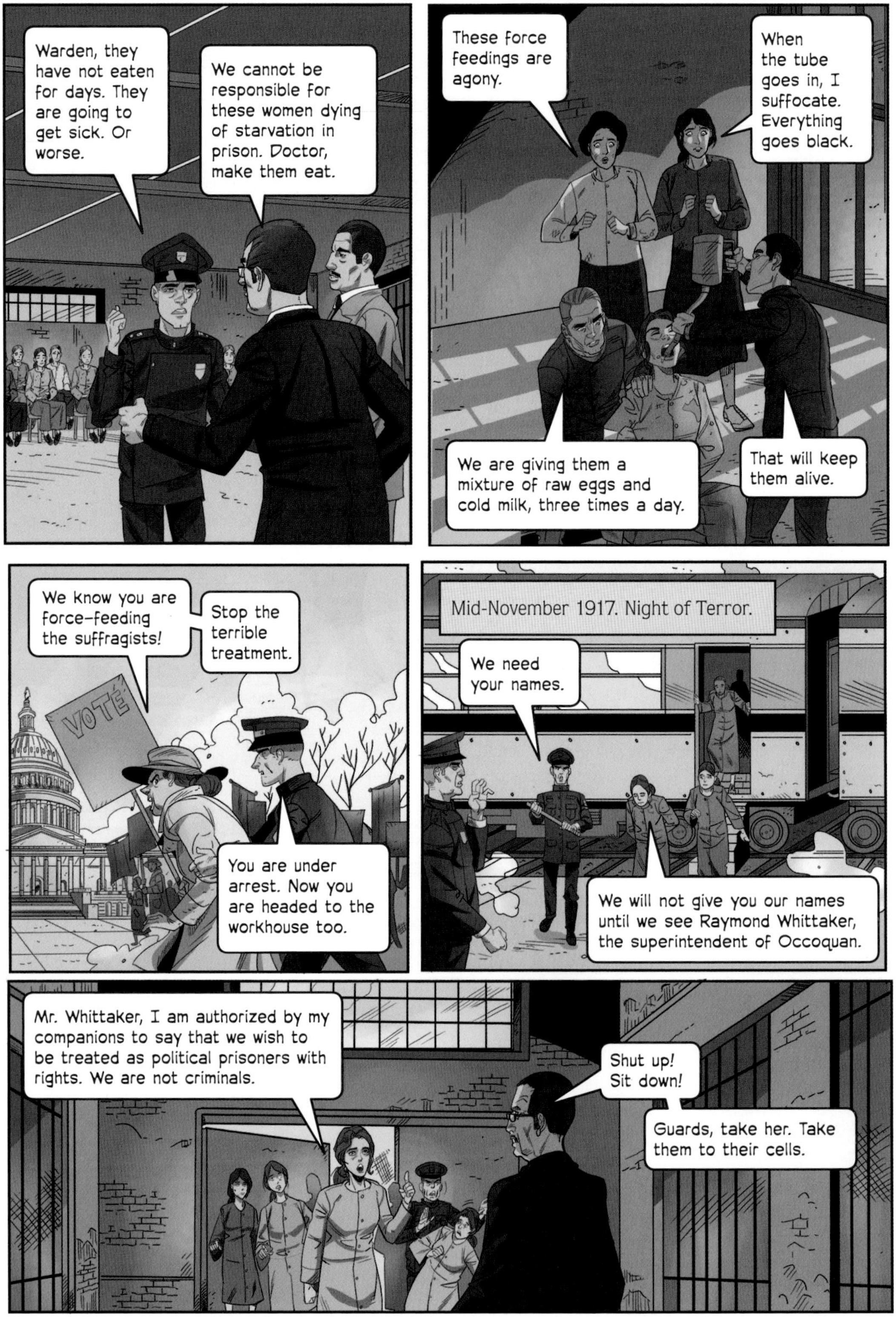
Warden, they have not eaten for days. They are going to get sick. Or worse.
We cannot be responsible for these women dying of starvation in prison. Doctor, make them eat.
These force feedings are agony.
When the tube goes in, I suffocate. Everything goes black.
We are giving them a mixture of raw eggs and cold milk, three times a day.
That will keep them alive.
We know you are force-feeding the suffragists!
Stop the terrible treatment.
VOTE
You are under arrest. Now you are headed to the workhouse too.
Mid-November 1917. Night of Terror.
We need your names.
We will not give you our names until we see Raymond Whittaker, the superintendent of Occoquan.
Mr. Whittaker, I am authorized by my companions to say that we wish to be treated as political prisoners with rights. We are not criminals.
Shut up! Sit down!
Guards, take her. Take them to their cells.

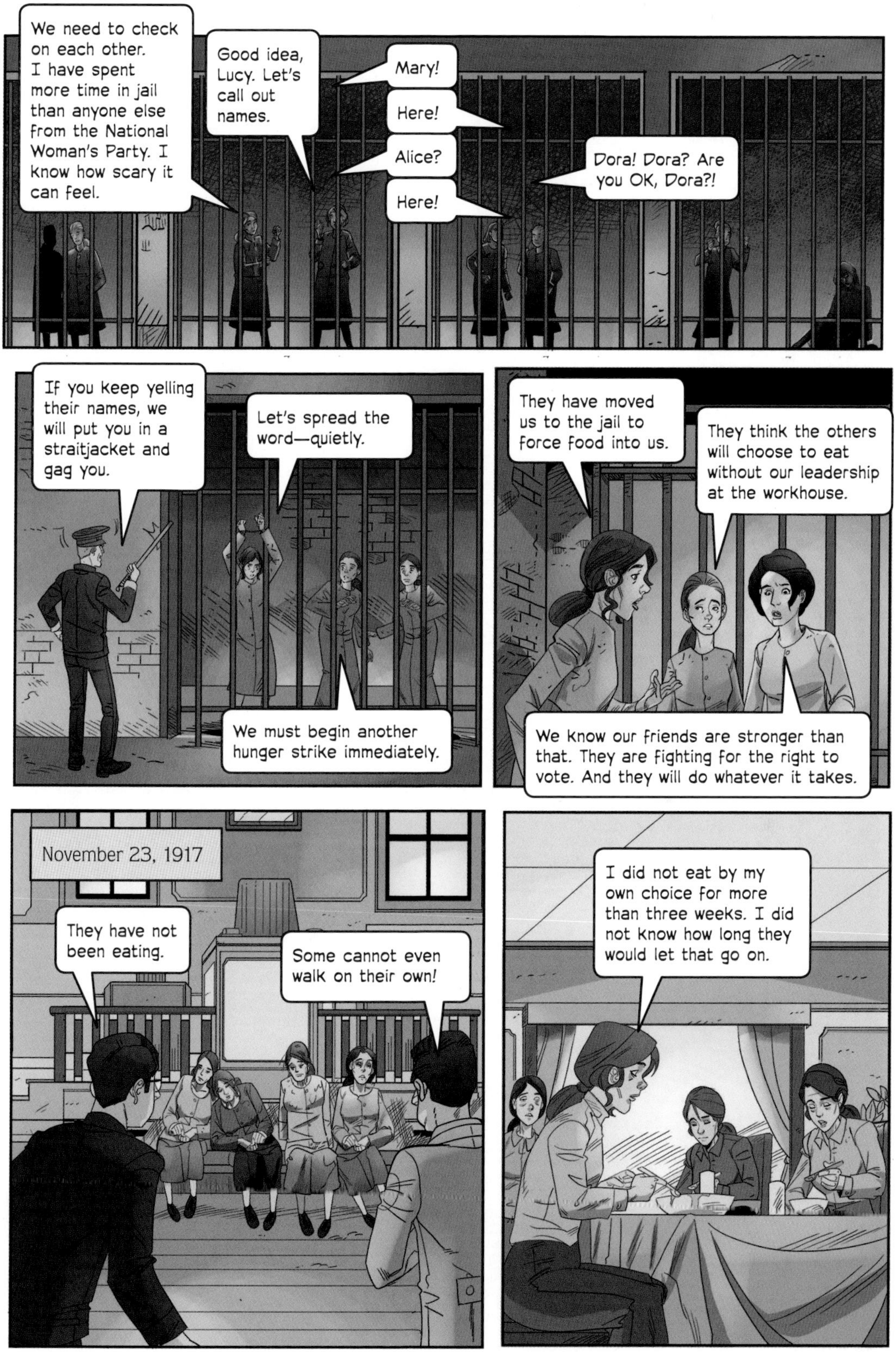
We need to check on each other. I have spent more time in jail than anyone else from the National Woman's Party. I know how scary it can feel.
Good idea, Lucy. Let's call out names.
Mary!
Here!
Alice?
Here!
Dora! Dora? Are you OK, Dora?!
If you keep yelling their names, we will put you in a straitjacket and gag you.
Let's spread the word—quietly.
We must begin another hunger strike immediately.
They have moved us to the jail to force food into us.
They think the others will choose to eat without our leadership at the workhouse.
We know our friends are stronger than that. They are fighting for the right to vote. And they will do whatever it takes.
November 23, 1917
They have not been eating.
Some cannot even walk on their own!
I did not eat by my own choice for more than three weeks. I did not know how long they would let that go on.

SHIFTING WINDS

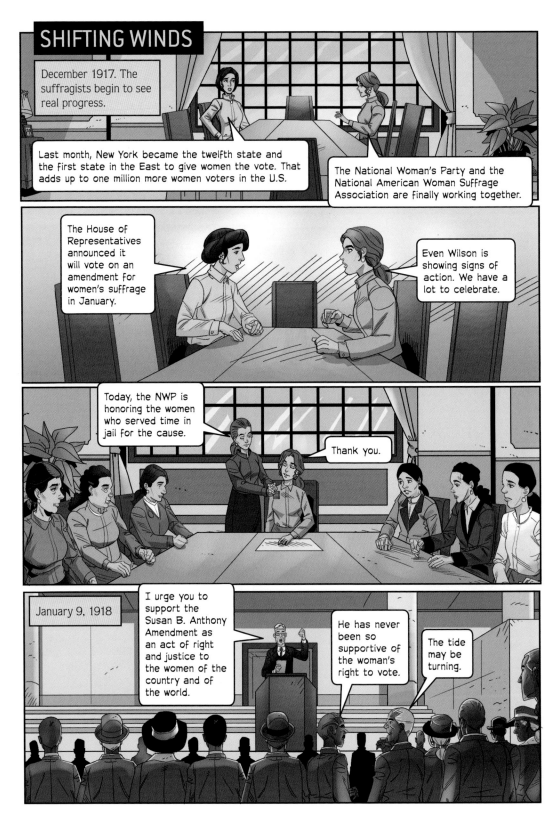

December 1917. The suffragists begin to see real progress.

Last month, New York became the twelfth state and the first state in the East to give women the vote. That adds up to one million more women voters in the U.S.

The National Woman's Party and the National American Woman Suffrage Association are finally working together.

The House of Representatives announced it will vote on an amendment for women's suffrage in January.

Even Wilson is showing signs of action. We have a lot to celebrate.

Today, the NWP is honoring the women who served time in jail for the cause.

Thank you.

January 9, 1918

I urge you to support the Susan B. Anthony Amendment as an act of right and justice to the women of the country and of the world.

He has never been so supportive of the woman's right to vote.

The tide may be turning.

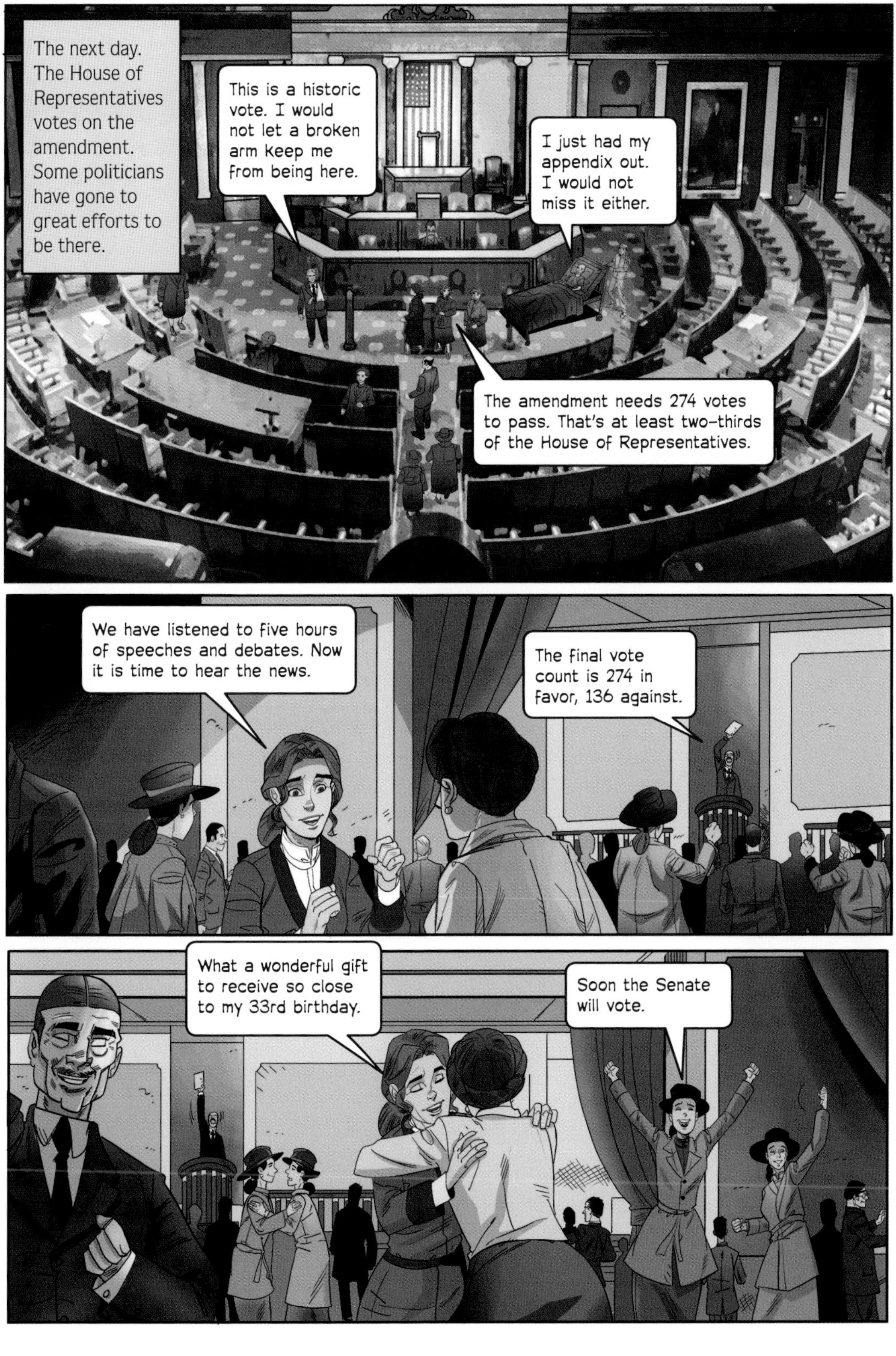
The next day. The House of Representatives votes on the amendment. Some politicians have gone to great efforts to be there.
This is a historic vote. I would not let a broken arm keep me from being here.
I just had my appendix out. I would not miss it either.
The amendment needs 274 votes to pass. That's at least two-thirds of the House of Representatives.
We have listened to five hours of speeches and debates. Now it is time to hear the news.
The final vote count is 274 in favor, 136 against.
What a wonderful gift to receive so close to my 33rd birthday.
Soon the Senate will vote.

A ROCKY ROAD TO CHANGE

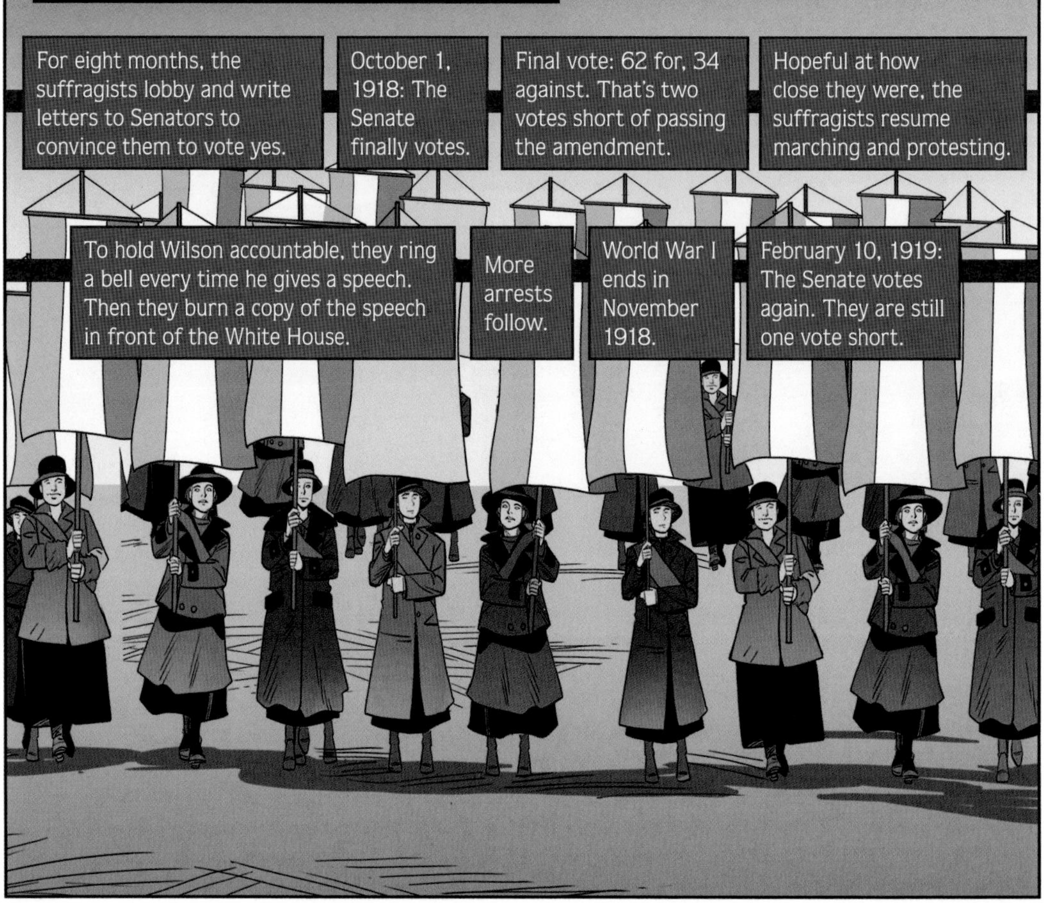
For eight months, the suffragists lobby and write letters to Senators to convince them to vote yes.
October 1, 1918: The Senate finally votes.
Final vote: 62 for, 34 against. That's two votes short of passing the amendment.
Hopeful at how close they were, the suffragists resume marching and protesting.
To hold Wilson accountable, they ring a bell every time he gives a speech. Then they burn a copy of the speech in front of the White House.
More arrests follow.
World War I ends in November 1918.
February 10, 1919: The Senate votes again. They are still one vote short.

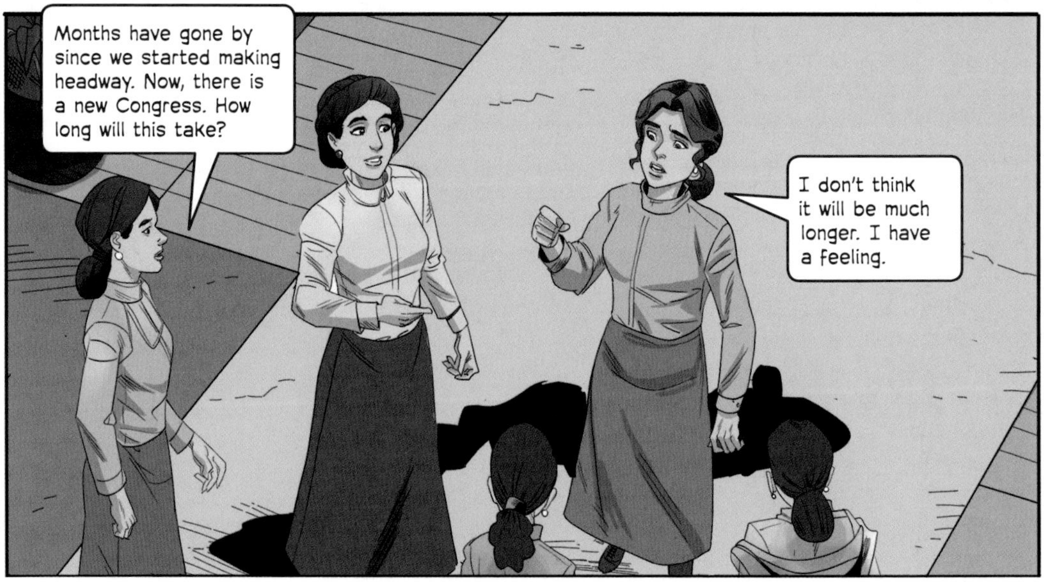
Months have gone by since we started making headway. Now, there is a new Congress. How long will this take?
I don't think it will be much longer. I have a feeling.

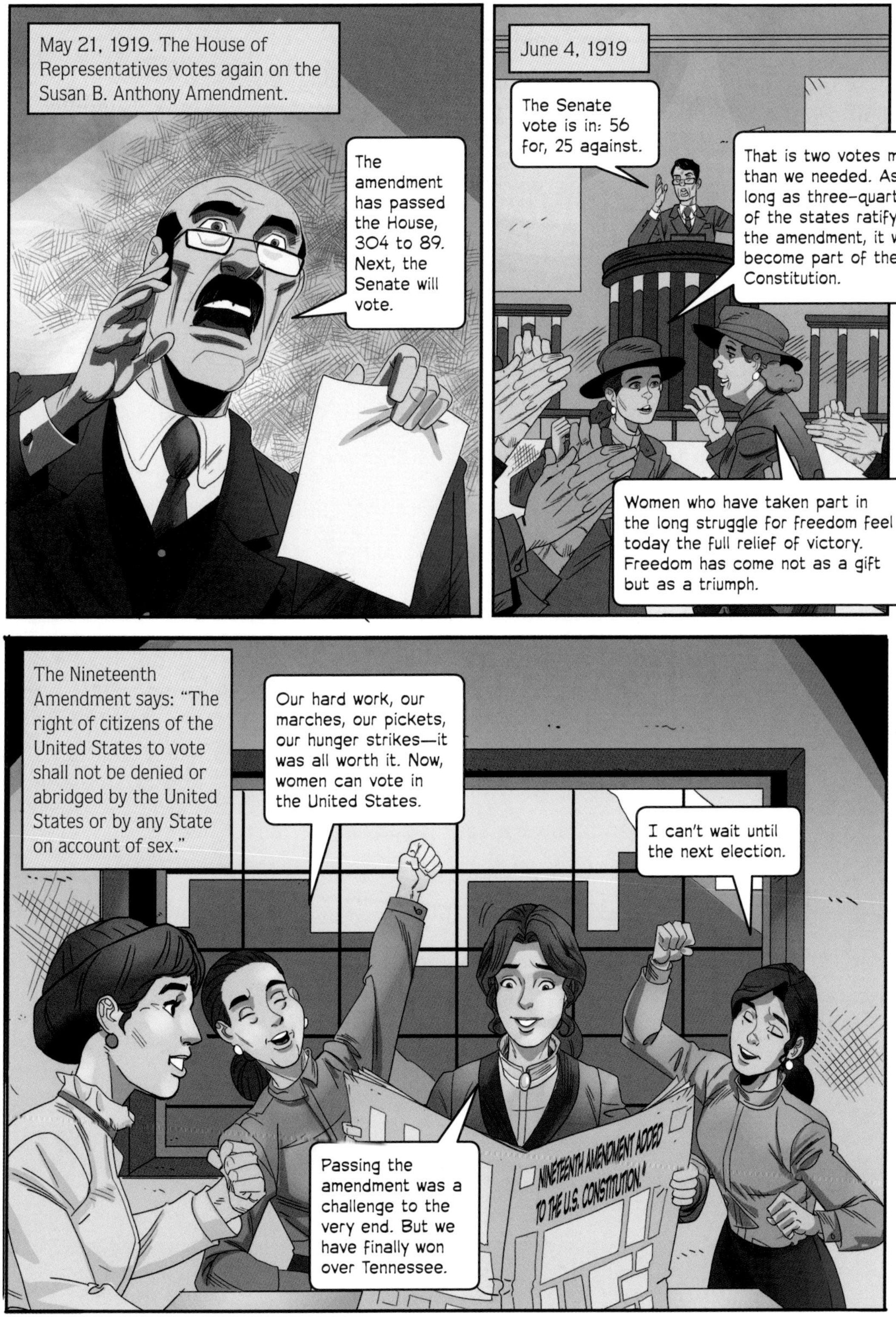
May 21, 1919. The House of Representatives votes again on the Susan B. Anthony Amendment.
The amendment has passed the House, 304 to 89. Next, the Senate will vote.
June 4, 1919
The Senate vote is in: 56 for, 25 against.
That is two votes more than we needed. As long as three-quarters of the states ratify the amendment, it will become part of the Constitution.
Women who have taken part in the long struggle for freedom feel today the full relief of victory. Freedom has come not as a gift but as a triumph.
The Nineteenth Amendment says: "The right of citizens of the United States to vote shall not be denied or abridged by the United States or by any State on account of sex."
Our hard work, our marches, our pickets, our hunger strikes—it was all worth it. Now, women can vote in the United States.
I can't wait until the next election.
Passing the amendment was a challenge to the very end. But we have finally won over Tennessee.
NINETEENTH AMENDMENT ADDED TO THE U.S. CONSTITUTION!

MORE ABOUT THE FIGHT FOR WOMEN'S SUFFRAGE

• Alice Paul was born on January 11, 1885, in New Jersey. Her father, a businessman, and mother were Quakers. They believed that women and men were equal, and that people should work to make society better. They lived a simple life and worked hard.

• As a child, Paul was a good student and loved to read. She played basketball, baseball, and field hockey.

• Paul went to England to study in 1907. Her experiences there shaped many of her opinions about the militant approach to the suffrage movement. She returned to the United States in 1910.

• Paul did not give up fighting for women's rights after the 19th Amendment passed. She spent the rest of her life working for more advances for women, including an amendment to the constitution that would give everyone the same rights and opportunities. Called the Equal Rights Amendment, it was passed by Congress in the early 1970s, but it was not approved by the number of states required to add it to the Constitution.

• Paul died on July 9, 1977, in New Jersey, just a few miles from where she was born.

• From the beginning of the suffrage movement, race has been a source of tension. Some of the most famous names in the suffrage movement include Susan B. Anthony, Elizabeth Cady Stanton, and Alice Paul. They were all white. Black men and women who fought just as hard for women's rights include Frederick Douglass, Ida B. Wells, and Mary Church Terrell.

• In 1868, the 14th Amendment to the U.S. Constitution allowed black Americans to be citizens of the United States. The 15th Amendment, which passed in 1870, gave black men the right to vote. For decades afterward, some states found ways to prevent black people from voting.

• In 1965, the Voting Rights Act prevented states from using taxes and tests to keep black people from voting. Debates continue today about practices of discrimination that are embedded in the U.S. voting system.

• In 1972, the United States passed Title IX of the Education Amendments. Title IX made it illegal to exclude girls and women from educational programs and activities. Among other impacts, the law opened the floodgates for girls to play sports.

• The struggle for women's rights has had many ups and downs over the years. Around the world, women continue to face many barriers, including discrimination, violence, and less access to education. The fight goes on.

GLOSSARY

amendment (uh-MEND-muhnt)—a formal change made to a law or legal document, such as the U.S. Constitution

cohorts (KOH-horts)—companions or associates

Constitution (kahn-stuh-TOO-shuhn)—legal document that describes the basic form of the U.S. government and the rights of citizens

gender equality (JEHN-dur i-KWAH-luh-tee)—the same rights for both males and females

inauguration (in-aw-guh-RAY-shuhn)—formal ceremony to swear a person into political office

leaflet (LEEF-lit)—a small flat or folded printed sheet given out to advertise or explain something

momentum (moh-MEN-tuhm)—movement forward

obstructing (ob-STRUHKT-ing)—making difficult to pass

petition (puh-TISH-uhn)—collection of signatures showing support for an issue

picketing (PIK-it-ing)—standing or walking outside a place to demand something

political party (puh-LIT-uh-kuhl PAR-tee)—a group of people who share the same beliefs about how the government should operate

politician (pol-uh-TISH-uhn)—someone who runs for or holds a government office

protester (PRO-tes-ter)—someone who publicly speaks out against something

radical (RAD-ih-kuhl)—extreme compared to what most people think or do

strategy (STRAT-uh-jee)—a careful plan or method

suffrage (SUHF-rij)—the right to vote

tactics (TAK-tiks)—actions planned to get specific results

READ MORE

Bartoletti, Susan Campbell. *How Women Won the Vote: Alice Paul, Lucy Burns, and Their Big Idea.* New York: Harper Collins, 2020.

Gillibrand, Kirsten. *Bold & Brave: Ten Heroes Who Won Women the Right to Vote.* New York: Alfred A. Knopf, 2018.

Stanborough, Rebecca. *A Women's Suffrage Time Capsule: Artifacts of the Movement for Voting Rights.* North Mankato, MN: Capstone, 2021.

INTERNET SITES

Civil Rights: Women's Suffrage
https://www.ducksters.com/history/civil_rights/womens_suffrage.php

For Kids! Women's History
https://www.nps.gov/subjects/womenshistory/for-kids.htm

Women's Suffrage
https://www.historyforkids.net/womens-suffrage.html

INDEX